Othello

By William Shakespeare

(Student Edition & Annotation Workbook)

The works enclosed within are available in the public domain. This edition is

intended to facilitated note taking and annotation for students.

Pearl Forest Publishing

<u>NOTES</u>

__NOTES__

Characters

OTHELLO, a Moorish general in the Venetian army

DESDEMONA, a Venetian lady

BRABANTIO, a Venetian senator, father to Desdemona

IAGO, Othello's standard-bearer, or "ancient"

EMILIA, Iago's wife and Desdemona's attendant

CASSIO, Othello's second-in-command, or lieutenant

RODERIGO, a Venetian gentleman

Duke of Venice

Venetian gentlemen, kinsmen to Brabantio:

LODOVICO

GRATIANO

Venetian senators

MONTANO, an official in Cyprus

BIANCA, a woman in Cyprus in love with Cassio

NOTES

Clown, a comic servant to Othello and Desdemona

Gentlemen of Cyprus

Sailors

Servants

Attendants

Officers

Messengers

Herald

Musicians

Torchbearers

NOTES

ACT 1

Scene 1

Enter Roderigo and Iago.

RODERIGO

    Tush, never tell me! I take it much unkindly

    That thou, Iago, who hast had my purse

    As if the strings were thine, shouldst know of this.

IAGO 'Sblood, but you'll not hear me!

    If ever I did dream of such a matter,   5

    Abhor me.

RODERIGO

    Thou toldst me thou didst hold him in thy hate.

IAGO Despise me

    If I do not. Three great ones of the city,

    In personal suit to make me his lieutenant,   10

    Off-capped to him; and, by the faith of man,

    I know my price, I am worth no worse a place.

    But he, as loving his own pride and purposes,

    Evades them with a bombast circumstance,

NOTES

4

Horribly stuffed with epithets of war,   15

And in conclusion,

Nonsuits my mediators. For "Certes," says he,   *fosh wood*

"I have already chose my officer."

And what was he?

Forsooth, a great arithmetician,   20

One Michael Cassio, a Florentine,

A fellow almost damned in a fair wife,

That never set a squadron in the field,

Nor the division of a battle knows

More than a spinster—unless the bookish theoric,   25

Wherein the togèd consuls can propose

As masterly as he. Mere prattle without practice

Is all his soldiership. But he, sir, had th' election;

And I, of whom his eyes had seen the proof

At Rhodes, at Cyprus, and on other grounds   30

Christened and heathen, must be beleed and

   calmed

By debitor and creditor. This countercaster,

He, in good time, must his lieutenant be,

And I, God bless the mark, his Moorship's ancient.   35

NOTES

RODERIGO

By heaven, I rather would have been his hangman.

IAGO

Why, there's no remedy. 'Tis the curse of service.

Preferment goes by letter and affection,

And not by old gradation, where each second

Stood heir to th' first. Now, sir, be judge yourself   40

Whether I in any just term am affined

To love the Moor.

RODERIGO

I would not follow him, then.

IAGO O, sir, content you.

I follow him to serve my turn upon him.   45

We cannot all be masters, nor all masters

Cannot be truly followed. You shall mark

Many a duteous and knee-crooking knave

That, doting on his own obsequious bondage,

Wears out his time, much like his master's ass,   50

For naught but provender, and when he's old,

    cashiered.

Whip me such honest knaves! Others there are

Who, trimmed in forms and visages of duty,

NOTES

Keep yet their hearts attending on themselves,   55

And, throwing but shows of service on their lords,

Do well thrive by them; and when they have lined

   their coats,

Do themselves homage. These fellows have some

   soul,   60

And such a one do I profess myself. For, sir,

It is as sure as you are Roderigo,

Were I the Moor I would not be Iago.

In following him, I follow but myself.

Heaven is my judge, not I for love and duty,   65

But seeming so for my peculiar end.

For when my outward action doth demonstrate

The native act and figure of my heart

In complement extern, 'tis not long after

But I will wear my heart upon my sleeve   70

For daws to peck at. I am not what I am.

RODERIGO

What a full fortune does the thick-lips owe

If he can carry 't thus!

IAGO Call up her father.

Rouse him. Make after him, poison his delight,   75

NOTES

Proclaim him in the streets; incense her kinsmen,

And, though he in a fertile climate dwell,

Plague him with flies. Though that his joy be joy,

Yet throw such chances of vexation on 't

As it may lose some color.   80

RODERIGO

Here is her father's house. I'll call aloud.

IAGO

Do, with like timorous accent and dire yell

As when, by night and negligence, the fire

Is spied in populous cities.

RODERIGO

What ho, Brabantio! Signior Brabantio, ho!   85

IAGO

Awake! What ho, Brabantio! Thieves, thieves!

Look to your house, your daughter, and your bags!

Thieves, thieves!

Enter Brabantio, above.

BRABANTIO

What is the reason of this terrible summons?

_____

NOTES

What is the matter there?   90

RODERIGO

   Signior, is all your family within?

IAGO

   Are your doors locked?

BRABANTIO Why, wherefore ask you this?

IAGO

   Zounds, sir, you're robbed. For shame, put on your

     gown!   95

   Your heart is burst. You have lost half your soul.

   Even now, now, very now, an old black ram

   Is tupping your white ewe. Arise, arise!

   Awake the snorting citizens with the bell,

   Or else the devil will make a grandsire of you.   100

   Arise, I say!

BRABANTIO What, have you lost your wits?

RODERIGO

   Most reverend signior, do you know my voice?

BRABANTIO Not I. What are you?

RODERIGO

   My name is Roderigo.   105

NOTES

BRABANTIO The worser welcome.

    I have charged thee not to haunt about my doors.

    In honest plainness thou hast heard me say

    My daughter is not for thee. And now in madness,

    Being full of supper and distemp'ring draughts,   110

    Upon malicious bravery dost thou come

    To start my quiet.

RODERIGO Sir, sir, sir—

BRABANTIO But thou must needs be sure

    My spirit and my place have in them power   115

    To make this bitter to thee.

RODERIGO

    Patience, good sir.

BRABANTIO What tell'st thou me of robbing?

    This is Venice. My house is not a grange.

RODERIGO Most grave Brabantio,   120

    In simple and pure soul I come to you—

IAGO Zounds, sir, you are one of those that will not

    serve God if the devil bid you. Because we come to

    do you service and you think we are ruffians, you'll

    have your daughter covered with a Barbary horse,   125

    you'll have your nephews neigh to you, you'll have

NOTES

coursers for cousins and jennets for germans.

BRABANTIO What profane wretch art thou?

IAGO I am one, sir, that comes to tell you your daughter

and the Moor are now making the beast with   130

two backs.

BRABANTIO Thou art a villain.

IAGO You are a senator.

BRABANTIO

This thou shalt answer. I know thee, Roderigo.

RODERIGO

Sir, I will answer anything. But I beseech you,   135

If 't be your pleasure and most wise consent—

As partly I find it is—that your fair daughter,

At this odd-even and dull watch o' th' night,

Transported with no worse nor better guard

But with a knave of common hire, a gondolier,   140

To the gross clasps of a lascivious Moor:

If this be known to you, and your allowance,

We then have done you bold and saucy wrongs.

But if you know not this, my manners tell me

We have your wrong rebuke. Do not believe   145

That from the sense of all civility

NOTES

I thus would play and trifle with your Reverence.

Your daughter, if you have not given her leave,

I say again, hath made a gross revolt,

Tying her duty, beauty, wit, and fortunes   150

In an extravagant and wheeling stranger

Of here and everywhere. Straight satisfy yourself.

If she be in her chamber or your house,

Let loose on me the justice of the state

For thus deluding you.   155

BRABANTIO Strike on the tinder, ho!

Give me a taper. Call up all my people.

This accident is not unlike my dream.

Belief of it oppresses me already.

Light, I say, light!   *He exits.* 160

IAGO, *to Roderigo* Farewell, for I must leave you.

It seems not meet nor wholesome to my place

To be producted, as if I stay I shall,

Against the Moor. For I do know the state,

However this may gall him with some check,   165

Cannot with safety cast him, for he's embarked

With such loud reason to the Cyprus wars,

Which even now stands in act, that, for their souls,

NOTES

Another of his fathom they have none

To lead their business. In which regard,   170

Though I do hate him as I do hell pains,

Yet, for necessity of present life,

I must show out a flag and sign of love—

Which is indeed but sign. That you shall surely find

   him,   175

Lead to the Sagittary the raisèd search,

And there will I be with him. So, farewell.   *He exits.*

Enter Brabantio in his nightgown, with Servants and

Torches.

BRABANTIO

It is too true an evil. Gone she is,

And what's to come of my despisèd time

Is naught but bitterness.—Now, Roderigo,   180

Where didst thou see her?—O, unhappy girl!—

With the Moor, sayst thou?—Who would be a

   father?—

How didst thou know 'twas she?—O, she deceives

   me   185

<u>NOTES</u>

Past thought!—What said she to you?—Get more

  tapers.

Raise all my kindred.—Are they married, think

  you?

RODERIGO Truly, I think they are.   190

BRABANTIO

O heaven! How got she out? O treason of the blood!

Fathers, from hence trust not your daughters' minds

By what you see them act.—Is there not charms

By which the property of youth and maidhood

May be abused? Have you not read, Roderigo,   195

Of some such thing?

RODERIGO Yes, sir, I have indeed.

BRABANTIO

Call up my brother.—O, would you had had her!—

Some one way, some another.—Do you know

Where we may apprehend her and the Moor?   200

RODERIGO

I think I can discover him, if you please

To get good guard and go along with me.

NOTES

BRABANTIO

Pray you lead on. At every house I'll call.

I may command at most.—Get weapons, ho!

And raise some special officers of night.—   205

On, good Roderigo. I will deserve your pains.

They exit.

NOTES

Scene 2

Enter Othello, Iago, Attendants, with Torches.

IAGO

    Though in the trade of war I have slain men,

    Yet do I hold it very stuff o' th' conscience

    To do no contrived murder. I lack iniquity

    Sometimes to do me service. Nine or ten times

    I had thought t' have yerked him here under the   5

       ribs.

OTHELLO

    'Tis better as it is.

IAGO Nay, but he prated

    And spoke such scurvy and provoking terms

    Against your Honor,   10

    That with the little godliness I have

    I did full hard forbear him. But I pray you, sir,

    Are you fast married? Be assured of this,

    That the magnifico is much beloved,

    And hath in his effect a voice potential   15

    As double as the Duke's. He will divorce you

    Or put upon you what restraint or grievance

NOTES

The law (with all his might to enforce it on)

Will give him cable.

OTHELLO Let him do his spite.   20

My services which I have done the signiory

Shall out-tongue his complaints. 'Tis yet to know

(Which, when I know that boasting is an honor,

I shall promulgate) I fetch my life and being

From men of royal siege, and my demerits   25

May speak unbonneted to as proud a fortune

As this that I have reached. For know, Iago,

But that I love the gentle Desdemona,

I would not my unhousèd free condition

Put into circumscription and confine   30

For the sea's worth. But look, what lights come

  yond?

IAGO

Those are the raisèd father and his friends.

You were best go in.

OTHELLO Not I. I must be found.   35

My parts, my title, and my perfect soul

Shall manifest me rightly. Is it they?

IAGO By Janus, I think no.

NOTES

Enter Cassio, with Officers, and Torches.

OTHELLO

    The servants of the Duke and my lieutenant!

    The goodness of the night upon you, friends.   40

    What is the news?

CASSIO The Duke does greet you, general,

    And he requires your haste-post-haste appearance,

    Even on the instant.

OTHELLO What is the matter, think you?   45

CASSIO

    Something from Cyprus, as I may divine.

    It is a business of some heat. The galleys

    Have sent a dozen sequent messengers

    This very night at one another's heels,

    And many of the Consuls, raised and met,   50

    Are at the Duke's already. You have been hotly

      called for.

    When, being not at your lodging to be found,

    The Senate hath sent about three several quests

    To search you out.   55

NOTES

OTHELLO 'Tis well I am found by you.

I will but spend a word here in the house

And go with you.   *He exits.*

CASSIO Ancient, what makes he here?

IAGO

Faith, he tonight hath boarded a land carrack.   60

If it prove lawful prize, he's made forever.

CASSIO

I do not understand.

IAGO He's married.

CASSIO To who?

IAGO

Marry, to—   65

Reenter Othello.

Come, captain, will you go?

OTHELLO Have with you.

CASSIO

Here comes another troop to seek for you.

Enter Brabantio, Roderigo, with Officers, and Torches.

NOTES

IAGO

It is Brabantio. General, be advised,

He comes to bad intent.   70

OTHELLO Holla, stand there!

RODERIGO

Signior, it is the Moor.

BRABANTIO Down with him,

   thief!

They draw their swords.

IAGO

You, Roderigo! Come, sir, I am for you.   75

OTHELLO

Keep up your bright swords, for the dew will rust

   them.

Good signior, you shall more command with years

Than with your weapons.

BRABANTIO

O, thou foul thief, where hast thou stowed my   80

   daughter?

Damned as thou art, thou hast enchanted her!

For I'll refer me to all things of sense,

NOTES

If she in chains of magic were not bound,

Whether a maid so tender, fair, and happy,   85

So opposite to marriage that she shunned

The wealthy curlèd darlings of our nation,

Would ever have, t' incur a general mock,

Run from her guardage to the sooty bosom   *racism*

Of such a thing as thou—to fear, not to delight!   90

Judge me the world, if 'tis not gross in sense

That thou hast practiced on her with foul charms,   *black magic*

Abused her delicate youth with drugs or minerals

That weakens motion. I'll have 't disputed on.

'Tis probable, and palpable to thinking.   95

I therefore apprehend and do attach thee

For an abuser of the world, a practicer

Of arts inhibited and out of warrant.—

Lay hold upon him. If he do resist,

Subdue him at his peril.   100

OTHELLO Hold your hands,

Both you of my inclining and the rest.

Were it my cue to fight, I should have known it

Without a prompter.—Whither will you that I go

To answer this your charge?   105

NOTES

BRABANTIO To prison, till fit time

    Of law and course of direct session

    Call thee to answer.

OTHELLO What if I do obey?

    How may the Duke be therewith satisfied,   110

    Whose messengers are here about my side,

    Upon some present business of the state,

    To bring me to him?

OFFICER 'Tis true, most worthy signior.

    The Duke's in council, and your noble self   115

    I am sure is sent for.

BRABANTIO How? The Duke in council?

    In this time of the night? Bring him away;

    Mine's not an idle cause. The Duke himself,

    Or any of my brothers of the state,   120

    Cannot but feel this wrong as 'twere their own.

    For if such actions may have passage free,

    Bondslaves and pagans shall our statesmen be.

They exit.

NOTES

Scene 3

Enter Duke, Senators, and Officers.

DUKE, *reading a paper*

There's no composition in these news

That gives them credit.

FIRST SENATOR, *reading a paper*

Indeed, they are disproportioned.

My letters say a hundred and seven galleys.

DUKE

And mine, a hundred forty.   5

SECOND SENATOR, *reading a paper*

And mine, two hundred.

But though they jump not on a just account

(As in these cases, where the aim reports

'Tis oft with difference), yet do they all confirm

A Turkish fleet, and bearing up to Cyprus.   10

DUKE

Nay, it is possible enough to judgment.

I do not so secure me in the error,

But the main article I do approve

In fearful sense.

NOTES

SAILOR, *within* What ho, what ho, what ho! 15

Enter Sailor.

OFFICER A messenger from the galleys.

DUKE Now, what's the business?

SAILOR

    The Turkish preparation makes for Rhodes.

    So was I bid report here to the state

    By Signior Angelo.   *He exits.* 20

DUKE

    How say you by this change?

FIRST SENATOR This cannot be,

    By no assay of reason. 'Tis a pageant

    To keep us in false gaze. When we consider

    Th' importancy of Cyprus to the Turk,   25

    And let ourselves again but understand

    That, as it more concerns the Turk than Rhodes,

    So may he with more facile question bear it,

    For that it stands not in such warlike brace,

    But altogether lacks th' abilities   30

    That Rhodes is dressed in—if we make thought of

NOTES

this,

We must not think the Turk is so unskillful

To leave that latest which concerns him first,

Neglecting an attempt of ease and gain   35

To wake and wage a danger profitless.

DUKE

Nay, in all confidence, he's not for Rhodes.

OFFICER Here is more news.

Enter a Messenger.

MESSENGER

The Ottomites, Reverend and Gracious,

Steering with due course toward the isle of Rhodes,   40

Have there injointed them with an after fleet.

FIRST SENATOR

Ay, so I thought. How many, as you guess?

MESSENGER

Of thirty sail; and now they do restem

Their backward course, bearing with frank

   appearance   45

Their purposes toward Cyprus. Signior Montano,

<u>NOTES</u>

Your trusty and most valiant servitor,

With his free duty recommends you thus,

And prays you to believe him.   *He exits.*

DUKE 'Tis certain, then, for Cyprus.   50

Marcus Luccicos, is not he in town?

FIRST SENATOR

He's now in Florence.

DUKE Write from us to him.

Post-post-haste. Dispatch.

FIRST SENATOR

Here comes Brabantio and the valiant Moor.   55

Enter Brabantio, Othello, Cassio, Iago, Roderigo, and

Officers.

DUKE

Valiant Othello, we must straight employ you

Against the general enemy Ottoman.

To Brabantio. I did not see you. Welcome, gentle

signior.

We lacked your counsel and your help tonight.   60

NOTES

BRABANTIO

So did I yours. Good your Grace, pardon me.

Neither my place nor aught I heard of business

Hath raised me from my bed, nor doth the general

  care

Take hold on me, for my particular grief   65

Is of so floodgate and o'erbearing nature

That it engluts and swallows other sorrows

And it is still itself.

DUKE Why, what's the matter?

BRABANTIO

My daughter! O, my daughter!   70

FIRST SENATOR Dead?

BRABANTIO Ay, to me.

She is abused, stol'n from me, and corrupted

By spells and medicines bought of mountebanks;

For nature so prepost'rously to err—   75

Being not deficient, blind, or lame of sense—

Sans witchcraft could not.

DUKE

Whoe'er he be that in this foul proceeding

Hath thus beguiled your daughter of herself

NOTES

And you of her, the bloody book of law   80

You shall yourself read in the bitter letter,

After your own sense, yea, though our proper son

Stood in your action.

BRABANTIO Humbly I thank your Grace.

Here is the man—this Moor, whom now it seems   85

Your special mandate for the state affairs

Hath hither brought.

ALL We are very sorry for 't.

DUKE, *to Othello*

What, in your own part, can you say to this?

BRABANTIO Nothing, but this is so.   90

OTHELLO

Most potent, grave, and reverend signiors,

My very noble and approved good masters:

That I have ta'en away this old man's daughter,

It is most true; true I have married her.

The very head and front of my offending   95

Hath this extent, no more. Rude am I in my speech,

And little blessed with the soft phrase of peace;

For since these arms of mine had seven years' pith,

Till now some nine moons wasted, they have used

NOTES

Their dearest action in the tented field,   100

And little of this great world can I speak

More than pertains to feats of broil and battle.

And therefore little shall I grace my cause

In speaking for myself. Yet, by your gracious

   patience,   105

I will a round unvarnished tale deliver

Of my whole course of love—what drugs, what

   charms,

What conjuration, and what mighty magic

(For such proceeding I am charged withal)   110

I won his daughter.

BRABANTIO A maiden never bold,

   Of spirit so still and quiet that her motion

   Blushed at herself. And she, in spite of nature,

   Of years, of country, credit, everything,   115

   To fall in love with what she feared to look on!

   It is a judgment maimed and most imperfect

   That will confess perfection so could err

   Against all rules of nature, and must be driven

   To find out practices of cunning hell   120

   Why this should be. I therefore vouch again

NOTES

That with some mixtures powerful o'er the blood,

Or with some dram conjured to this effect,

He wrought upon her.

DUKE To vouch this is no proof   125

Without more wider and more overt test

Than these thin habits and poor likelihoods

Of modern seeming do prefer against him.

FIRST SENATOR But, Othello, speak:

Did you by indirect and forcèd courses   130

Subdue and poison this young maid's affections?

Or came it by request, and such fair question

As soul to soul affordeth?

OTHELLO I do beseech you,

Send for the lady to the Sagittary   135

And let her speak of me before her father.

If you do find me foul in her report,

The trust, the office I do hold of you,

Not only take away, but let your sentence

Even fall upon my life.   140

DUKE Fetch Desdemona hither.

OTHELLO

Ancient, conduct them. You best know the place.

NOTES

And till she come, as truly as to heaven

I do confess the vices of my blood,

So justly to your grave ears I'll present   145

How I did thrive in this fair lady's love,

And she in mine.

DUKE Say it, Othello.

OTHELLO

Her father loved me, oft invited me,

Still questioned me the story of my life   150

From year to year—the battles, sieges, fortunes

That I have passed.

I ran it through, even from my boyish days

To th' very moment that he bade me tell it,

Wherein I spoke of most disastrous chances: 155

Of moving accidents by flood and field,

Of hairbreadth 'scapes i' th' imminent deadly

   breach,

Of being taken by the insolent foe

And sold to slavery, of my redemption thence,   160

And portance in my traveler's history,

Wherein of antres vast and deserts idle,

NOTES

Rough quarries, rocks, and hills whose heads

  touch heaven,

It was my hint to speak—such was my process—   165

And of the cannibals that each other eat,

The Anthropophagi, and men whose heads

Do grow beneath their shoulders. These things to

  hear

Would Desdemona seriously incline.   170

But still the house affairs would draw her thence,

Which ever as she could with haste dispatch

She'd come again, and with a greedy ear

Devour up my discourse. Which I, observing,

Took once a pliant hour, and found good means   175

To draw from her a prayer of earnest heart

That I would all my pilgrimage dilate,

Whereof by parcels she had something heard,

But not intentively. I did consent,

And often did beguile her of her tears   180

When I did speak of some distressful stroke

That my youth suffered. My story being done,

She gave me for my pains a world of sighs.

She swore, in faith, 'twas strange, 'twas passing

NOTES

strange, 185

'Twas pitiful, 'twas wondrous pitiful.

She wished she had not heard it, yet she wished

That heaven had made her such a man. She thanked

me,

And bade me, if I had a friend that loved her, 190

I should but teach him how to tell my story,

And that would woo her. Upon this hint I spake.

She loved me for the dangers I had passed,

And I loved her that she did pity them.

This only is the witchcraft I have used. 195

Here comes the lady. Let her witness it.

Enter Desdemona, Iago, Attendants.

DUKE

I think this tale would win my daughter, too.

Good Brabantio,

Take up this mangled matter at the best.

Men do their broken weapons rather use 200

Than their bare hands.

BRABANTIO I pray you hear her speak.

NOTES

If she confess that she was half the wooer,

Destruction on my head if my bad blame

Light on the man.—Come hither, gentle mistress.   205

Do you perceive in all this noble company

Where most you owe obedience?

DESDEMONA My noble father,

I do perceive here a divided duty.

To you I am bound for life and education.   210

My life and education both do learn me

How to respect you. You are the lord of duty.

I am hitherto your daughter. But here's my

    husband.

And so much duty as my mother showed   215

To you, preferring you before her father,

So much I challenge that I may profess

Due to the Moor my lord.

BRABANTIO God be with you! I have done.

Please it your Grace, on to the state affairs.   220

I had rather to adopt a child than get it.—

Come hither, Moor.

I here do give thee that with all my heart

Which, but thou hast already, with all my heart

NOTES

I would keep from thee.—For your sake, jewel,   225

I am glad at soul I have no other child,

For thy escape would teach me tyranny,

To hang clogs on them.—I have done, my lord.

DUKE

Let me speak like yourself and lay a sentence,

Which as a grise or step may help these lovers   230

Into your favor.

When remedies are past, the griefs are ended

By seeing the worst, which late on hopes depended.

To mourn a mischief that is past and gone

Is the next way to draw new mischief on.   235

What cannot be preserved when fortune takes,

Patience her injury a mock'ry makes.

The robbed that smiles steals something from the

   thief;

He robs himself that spends a bootless grief.   240

BRABANTIO

So let the Turk of Cyprus us beguile,

We lose it not so long as we can smile.

He bears the sentence well that nothing bears

But the free comfort which from thence he hears;

NOTES

But he bears both the sentence and the sorrow   245

That, to pay grief, must of poor patience borrow.

These sentences to sugar or to gall,

Being strong on both sides, are equivocal.

But words are words. I never yet did hear

That the bruisèd heart was piercèd through the   250

   ear.

I humbly beseech you, proceed to th' affairs of

   state.

DUKE The Turk with a most mighty preparation makes

   for Cyprus. Othello, the fortitude of the place is   255

   best known to you. And though we have there a

   substitute of most allowed sufficiency, yet opinion, a

   sovereign mistress of effects, throws a more safer

   voice on you. You must therefore be content to

   slubber the gloss of your new fortunes with this   260

   more stubborn and boist'rous expedition.

OTHELLO

The tyrant custom, most grave senators,

Hath made the flinty and steel couch of war

My thrice-driven bed of down. I do agnize

A natural and prompt alacrity   265

NOTES

I find in hardness, and do undertake

This present wars against the Ottomites.

Most humbly, therefore, bending to your state,

I crave fit disposition for my wife,

Due reference of place and exhibition,   270

With such accommodation and besort

As levels with her breeding.

DUKE

Why, at her father's.

BRABANTIO I will not have it so.

OTHELLO Nor I.   275

DESDEMONA Nor would I there reside

To put my father in impatient thoughts

By being in his eye. Most gracious duke,

To my unfolding lend your prosperous ear

And let me find a charter in your voice   280

T' assist my simpleness.

DUKE What would you, Desdemona?

DESDEMONA

That I love the Moor to live with him

My downright violence and storm of fortunes

May trumpet to the world. My heart's subdued   285

NOTES

Even to the very quality of my lord.

I saw Othello's visage in his mind,

And to his honors and his valiant parts

Did I my soul and fortunes consecrate.

So that, dear lords, if I be left behind,   290

A moth of peace, and he go to the war,

The rites for why I love him are bereft me

And I a heavy interim shall support

By his dear absence. Let me go with him.

OTHELLO Let her have your voice.   295

Vouch with me, heaven, I therefore beg it not

To please the palate of my appetite,

Nor to comply with heat (the young affects

In me defunct) and proper satisfaction,

But to be free and bounteous to her mind.   300

And heaven defend your good souls that you think

I will your serious and great business scant

For she is with me. No, when light-winged toys

Of feathered Cupid seel with wanton dullness

My speculative and officed instruments,   305

That my disports corrupt and taint my business,

Let housewives make a skillet of my helm,

NOTES

And all indign and base adversities

Make head against my estimation.

DUKE

Be it as you shall privately determine,   310

Either for her stay or going. Th' affair cries haste,

And speed must answer it.

FIRST SENATOR

You must away tonight.

OTHELLO With all my

heart.   315

DUKE

At nine i' th' morning here we'll meet again.

Othello, leave some officer behind

And he shall our commission bring to you,

With such things else of quality and respect

As doth import you.   320

OTHELLO So please your Grace, my

ancient.

A man he is of honesty and trust.

To his conveyance I assign my wife,

With what else needful your good Grace shall think   325

To be sent after me.

NOTES

DUKE Let it be so.

    Good night to everyone. *To Brabantio.* And, noble

     signior,

    If virtue no delighted beauty lack,   330

    Your son-in-law is far more fair than black.

FIRST SENATOR

    Adieu, brave Moor, use Desdemona well.

BRABANTIO

    Look to her, Moor, if thou hast eyes to see.

    She has deceived her father, and may thee.   *He exits.*

OTHELLO

    My life upon her faith!   335

                        The Duke, the Senators, Cassio, and Officers exit.

    Honest Iago,

    My Desdemona must I leave to thee.

    I prithee let thy wife attend on her,

    And bring them after in the best advantage.—

    Come, Desdemona, I have but an hour   340

    Of love, of worldly matters, and direction

    To spend with thee. We must obey the time.

                        Othello and Desdemona exit.

RODERIGO Iago—

<u>NOTES</u>

IAGO What sayst thou, noble heart?

RODERIGO What will I do, think'st thou?   345

IAGO Why, go to bed and sleep.

RODERIGO I will incontinently drown myself.

IAGO If thou dost, I shall never love thee after. Why,

    thou silly gentleman!

RODERIGO It is silliness to live, when to live is torment,   350

    and then have we a prescription to die when death is

    our physician.

IAGO O, villainous! I have looked upon the world for

    four times seven years, and since I could distinguish

    betwixt a benefit and an injury, I never found   355

    man that knew how to love himself. Ere I would say

    I would drown myself for the love of a guinea hen, I

    would change my humanity with a baboon.

RODERIGO What should I do? I confess it is my shame

    to be so fond, but it is not in my virtue to amend it.   360

IAGO Virtue? A fig! 'Tis in ourselves that we are thus or

    thus. Our bodies are our gardens, to the which our

    wills are gardeners. So that if we will plant nettles

    or sow lettuce, set hyssop and weed up thyme,

    supply it with one gender of herbs or distract it   365

NOTES

with many, either to have it sterile with idleness or
manured with industry, why the power and corrigible
authority of this lies in our wills. If the balance
of our lives had not one scale of reason to poise
another of sensuality, the blood and baseness of our   370
natures would conduct us to most prepost'rous
conclusions. But we have reason to cool our raging
motions, our carnal stings, our unbitted lusts—
whereof I take this that you call love to be a sect, or
scion.   375

RODERIGO It cannot be.

IAGO It is merely a lust of the blood and a permission
of the will. Come, be a man! Drown thyself? Drown
cats and blind puppies. I have professed me thy
friend, and I confess me knit to thy deserving   380
with cables of perdurable toughness. I could never
better stead thee than now. Put money in thy purse.
Follow thou the wars; defeat thy favor with an
usurped beard. I say, put money in thy purse. It
cannot be that Desdemona should long continue   385
her love to the Moor—put money in thy purse—
nor he his to her. It was a violent commencement in

NOTES

her, and thou shalt see an answerable sequestration
—put but money in thy purse. These Moors are
changeable in their wills. Fill thy purse with money.   390
The food that to him now is as luscious as locusts
shall be to him shortly as bitter as coloquintida.
She must change for youth. When she is sated
with his body she will find the error of her choice.
Therefore, put money in thy purse. If thou wilt   395
needs damn thyself, do it a more delicate way than
drowning. Make all the money thou canst. If sanctimony
and a frail vow betwixt an erring barbarian
and a supersubtle Venetian be not too hard for my
wits and all the tribe of hell, thou shalt enjoy her.   400
Therefore make money. A pox of drowning thyself!
It is clean out of the way. Seek thou rather to be
hanged in compassing thy joy than to be drowned
and go without her.

RODERIGO Wilt thou be fast to my hopes if I depend on   405
the issue?

IAGO Thou art sure of me. Go, make money. I have
told thee often, and I retell thee again and again, I
hate the Moor. My cause is hearted; thine hath no

NOTES

less reason. Let us be conjunctive in our revenge   410

against him. If thou canst cuckold him, thou dost

thyself a pleasure, me a sport. There are many

events in the womb of time which will be delivered.

Traverse, go, provide thy money. We will have more

of this tomorrow. Adieu.   415

RODERIGO Where shall we meet i' th' morning?

IAGO At my lodging.

RODERIGO I'll be with thee betimes.

IAGO Go to, farewell. Do you hear, Roderigo?

RODERIGO What say you?   420

IAGO No more of drowning, do you hear?

RODERIGO I am changed.

IAGO Go to, farewell. Put money enough in your

   purse.

RODERIGO I'll sell all my land.   *He exits.* 425

IAGO

   Thus do I ever make my fool my purse.

   For I mine own gained knowledge should profane

   If I would time expend with such a snipe

   But for my sport and profit. I hate the Moor,

   And it is thought abroad that 'twixt my sheets   *othello slept with Iago wife?*   430

NOTES

'Has done my office. I know not if 't be true,

But I, for mere suspicion in that kind,

Will do as if for surety. He holds me well.

The better shall my purpose work on him.

Cassio's a proper man. Let me see now: 435

To get his place and to plume up my will

In double knavery—How? how?—Let's see.

After some time, to abuse Othello's ear   *Too familiar w/ desdemona*

That he is too familiar with his wife.

He hath a person and a smooth dispose   440

To be suspected, framed to make women false.

The Moor is of a free and open nature

That thinks men honest that but seem to be so,

And will as tenderly be led by th' nose

As asses are.   *Simile, animal, racism*   445

I have 't. It is engendered. Hell and night   *rhyme couplet*

Must bring this monstrous birth to the world's light.   *; watch use*

                                                    black & white   *He exits.*

NOTES

ACT 2

Scene 1

Enter Montano and two Gentlemen.

MONTANO

What from the cape can you discern at sea?

FIRST GENTLEMAN

Nothing at all. It is a high-wrought flood.

I cannot 'twixt the heaven and the main

Descry a sail.

MONTANO

Methinks the wind hath spoke aloud at land.   5

A fuller blast ne'er shook our battlements.

If it hath ruffianed so upon the sea,

What ribs of oak, when mountains melt on them,

Can hold the mortise? What shall we hear of this?

SECOND GENTLEMAN

A segregation of the Turkish fleet.   10

For do but stand upon the foaming shore,

The chidden billow seems to pelt the clouds,

NOTES

The wind-shaked surge, with high and monstrous

   mane,

Seems to cast water on the burning Bear   15

And quench the guards of th' ever-fixèd pole.

I never did like molestation view

On the enchafèd flood.

MONTANO If that the Turkish fleet

  Be not ensheltered and embayed, they are drowned.   20

  It is impossible to bear it out.

Enter a third Gentleman.

THIRD GENTLEMAN News, lads! Our wars are done.

  The desperate tempest hath so banged the Turks

  That their designment halts. A noble ship of Venice

  Hath seen a grievous wrack and sufferance   25

  On most part of their fleet.

MONTANO

  How? Is this true?

THIRD GENTLEMAN The ship is here put in,

  A Veronesa. Michael Cassio,

  Lieutenant to the warlike Moor Othello,   30

NOTES

Is come on shore; the Moor himself at sea,

And is in full commission here for Cyprus.

MONTANO

I am glad on 't. 'Tis a worthy governor.

THIRD GENTLEMAN

But this same Cassio, though he speak of comfort

Touching the Turkish loss, yet he looks sadly   35

And prays the Moor be safe, for they were parted

With foul and violent tempest.

MONTANO Pray heaven he be;

For I have served him, and the man commands

Like a full soldier. Let's to the seaside, ho!   40

As well to see the vessel that's come in

As to throw out our eyes for brave Othello,

Even till we make the main and th' aerial blue

An indistinct regard.

THIRD GENTLEMAN Come, let's do so;   45

For every minute is expectancy

Of more arrivance.

Enter Cassio.

NOTES

CASSIO

    Thanks, you the valiant of this warlike isle,

    That so approve the Moor! O, let the heavens

    Give him defense against the elements,   50

    For I have lost him on a dangerous sea.

MONTANO Is he well shipped?

CASSIO

    His bark is stoutly timbered, and his pilot

    Of very expert and approved allowance;

    Therefore my hopes, not surfeited to death,   55

    Stand in bold cure.

Voices cry within. "A sail, a sail, a sail!

"

Enter a Messenger.

CASSIO What noise?

MESSENGER

    The town is empty; on the brow o' th' sea

    Stand ranks of people, and they cry "A sail!"

CASSIO

    My hopes do shape him for the Governor.   60

A shot.

NOTES

SECOND GENTLEMAN

They do discharge their shot of courtesy.

Our friends, at least.

CASSIO I pray you, sir, go forth,

And give us truth who 'tis that is arrived.

SECOND GENTLEMAN I shall.   *He exits.* 65

MONTANO

But, good lieutenant, is your general wived?

CASSIO

Most fortunately. He hath achieved a maid

That paragons description and wild fame,

One that excels the quirks of blazoning pens,

And in th' essential vesture of creation   70

Does tire the ingener.

Enter Second Gentleman.

How now? Who has put in?

SECOND GENTLEMAN

'Tis one Iago, ancient to the General.

CASSIO

'Has had most favorable and happy speed!

NOTES

Tempests themselves, high seas, and howling winds,   75

The guttered rocks and congregated sands

(Traitors ensteeped to clog the guiltless keel),

As having sense of beauty, do omit

Their mortal natures, letting go safely by

The divine Desdemona.   80

MONTANO What is she?

CASSIO

She that I spake of, our great captain's captain,

Left in the conduct of the bold Iago,

Whose footing here anticipates our thoughts

A sennight's speed. Great Jove, Othello guard,   85

And swell his sail with thine own powerful breath,

That he may bless this bay with his tall ship,

Make love's quick pants in Desdemona's arms,

Give renewed fire to our extincted spirits,

And bring all Cyprus comfort!   90

Enter Desdemona, Iago, Roderigo, and Emilia.

O, behold,

The riches of the ship is come on shore!

NOTES

You men of Cyprus, let her have your knees.

He kneels.

Hail to thee, lady, and the grace of heaven,

Before, behind thee, and on every hand   95

Enwheel thee round.   *He rises.*

DESDEMONA I thank you, valiant Cassio.

What tidings can you tell of my lord?

CASSIO

He is not yet arrived, nor know I aught

But that he's well and will be shortly here.   100

DESDEMONA

O, but I fear—How lost you company?

CASSIO

The great contention of sea and skies

Parted our fellowship.

Within "A sail, a sail!" A shot.

But hark, a sail!

SECOND GENTLEMAN

They give their greeting to the citadel.   105

This likewise is a friend.

CASSIO See for the news.

Second Gentleman exits.

NOTES

Good ancient, you are welcome. Welcome, mistress.

He kisses Emilia.

Let it not gall your patience, good Iago,

That I extend my manners. 'Tis my breeding   110

That gives me this bold show of courtesy.

IAGO

Sir, would she give you so much of her lips

As of her tongue she oft bestows on me,

You would have enough.

DESDEMONA

Alas, she has no speech!   115

IAGO In faith, too much.

I find it still when I have list to sleep.

Marry, before your Ladyship, I grant,

She puts her tongue a little in her heart

And chides with thinking.   120

EMILIA You have little cause to say so.

IAGO Come on, come on! You are pictures out of door,

bells in your parlors, wildcats in your kitchens,

saints in your injuries, devils being offended, players

in your huswifery, and huswives in your beds.   125

DESDEMONA Oh, fie upon thee, slanderer.

NOTES

IAGO

Nay, it is true, or else I am a Turk.

You rise to play, and go to bed to work.

EMILIA

You shall not write my praise.

IAGO No, let me not.   130

DESDEMONA

What wouldst write of me if thou shouldst praise

me?

IAGO

O, gentle lady, do not put me to 't,

For I am nothing if not critical.

DESDEMONA

Come on, assay.—There's one gone to the harbor?   135

IAGO Ay, madam.

DESDEMONA, *aside*

I am not merry, but I do beguile

The thing I am by seeming otherwise.—

Come, how wouldst thou praise me?

IAGO I am about it, but indeed my invention comes   140

from my pate as birdlime does from frieze: it

plucks out brains and all. But my muse labors, and

NOTES

thus she is delivered:

> *If she be fair and wise, fairness and wit,*
>
> *The one's for use, the other useth it.* 145

DESDEMONA

Well praised! How if she be black and witty?

IAGO

> *If she be black, and thereto have a wit,*
>
> *She'll find a white that shall her blackness hit.*

DESDEMONA

Worse and worse.

EMILIA How if fair and foolish? 150

IAGO

> *She never yet was foolish that was fair,*
>
> *For even her folly helped her to an heir.*

DESDEMONA These are old fond paradoxes to make

fools laugh i' th' alehouse. What miserable praise

hast thou for her that's foul and foolish? 155

IAGO

> *There's none so foul and foolish thereunto,*
>
> *But does foul pranks which fair and wise ones do.*

DESDEMONA O heavy ignorance! Thou praisest the

worst best. But what praise couldst thou bestow on

NOTES

55

a deserving woman indeed, one that in the authority 160

of her merit did justly put on the vouch of very

malice itself?

IAGO

She that was ever fair and never proud,

Had tongue at will and yet was never loud,

Never lacked gold and yet went never gay, 165

Fled from her wish, and yet said "Now I may,"

She that being angered, her revenge being nigh,

Bade her wrong stay and her displeasure fly,

She that in wisdom never was so frail

To change the cod's head for the salmon's tail, 170

She that could think and ne'er disclose her mind,

See suitors following and not look behind,

She was a wight, if ever such wight were—

DESDEMONA To do what?

IAGO

To suckle fools and chronicle small beer. 175

DESDEMONA O, most lame and impotent conclusion!

—Do not learn of him, Emilia, though he be thy

husband.—How say you, Cassio? Is he not a most

profane and liberal counselor?

NOTES

CASSIO He speaks home, madam. You may relish him   180

    more in the soldier than in the scholar.

Cassio takes Desdemona's hand.

IAGO, *aside* He takes her by the palm. Ay, well said,

    whisper. With as little a web as this will I ensnare as

    great a fly as Cassio. Ay, smile upon her, do. I will

    gyve thee in thine own courtship. You say true, 'tis   185

    so indeed. If such tricks as these strip you out of

    your lieutenantry, it had been better you had not

    kissed your three fingers so oft, which now again

    you are most apt to play the sir in. Very good; well

    kissed; an excellent courtesy! 'Tis so, indeed. Yet   190

    again your fingers to your lips? Would they were

    clyster pipes for your sake!   *Trumpets within.*

    The Moor. I know his trumpet.

CASSIO 'Tis truly so.

DESDEMONA Let's meet him and receive him.   195

CASSIO Lo, where he comes!

Enter Othello and Attendants.

NOTES

OTHELLO

O, my fair warrior!

DESDEMONA My dear Othello!

OTHELLO

It gives me wonder great as my content

To see you here before me. O my soul's joy!   200

If after every tempest come such calms,

May the winds blow till they have wakened death,

And let the laboring bark climb hills of seas

Olympus high, and duck again as low

As hell's from heaven! If it were now to die,   205

'Twere now to be most happy, for I fear

My soul hath her content so absolute

That not another comfort like to this

Succeeds in unknown fate.

DESDEMONA The heavens forbid   210

But that our loves and comforts should increase

Even as our days do grow!

OTHELLO Amen to that, sweet powers!

I cannot speak enough of this content.

It stops me here; it is too much of joy.   *They kiss.* 215

And this, and this, the greatest discords be

NOTES

That e'er our hearts shall make!

IAGO, *aside* O, you are well tuned now,

    But I'll set down the pegs that make this music,

    As honest as I am.   220

OTHELLO Come. Let us to the castle.—

    News, friends! Our wars are done. The Turks are

      drowned.

    How does my old acquaintance of this isle?—

    Honey, you shall be well desired in Cyprus.   225

    I have found great love amongst them. O, my sweet,

    I prattle out of fashion, and I dote

    In mine own comforts.—I prithee, good Iago,

    Go to the bay and disembark my coffers.

    Bring thou the master to the citadel.   230

    He is a good one, and his worthiness

    Does challenge much respect.—Come, Desdemona.

    Once more, well met at Cyprus.

                                  All but Iago and Roderigo exit.

IAGO, *to a departing Attendant* Do thou meet me presently

    at the harbor. *To Roderigo.* Come hither. If   235

    thou be'st valiant—as they say base men being in

    love have then a nobility in their natures more than

NOTES

is native to them—list me. The Lieutenant tonight

watches on the court of guard. First, I must tell thee

this: Desdemona is directly in love with him.   240

RODERIGO With him? Why, 'tis not possible.

IAGO Lay thy finger thus, and let thy soul be instructed.

Mark me with what violence she first loved the

Moor but for bragging and telling her fantastical

lies. And will she love him still for prating? Let not   245

thy discreet heart think it. Her eye must be fed. And

what delight shall she have to look on the devil?

When the blood is made dull with the act of sport,

there should be, again to inflame it and to give

satiety a fresh appetite, loveliness in favor, sympathy   250

in years, manners, and beauties, all which the Moor

is defective in. Now, for want of these required

conveniences, her delicate tenderness will find itself

abused, begin to heave the gorge, disrelish and

abhor the Moor. Very nature will instruct her in it   255

and compel her to some second choice. Now, sir,

this granted—as it is a most pregnant and unforced

position—who stands so eminent in the degree of

this fortune as Cassio does? A knave very voluble, no

NOTES

further conscionable than in putting on the mere   260

form of civil and humane seeming for the better

compassing of his salt and most hidden loose

affection. Why, none, why, none! A slipper and

subtle knave, a finder-out of occasions, that has an

eye can stamp and counterfeit advantages, though   265

true advantage never present itself; a devilish knave!

Besides, the knave is handsome, young, and hath all

those requisites in him that folly and green minds

look after. A pestilent complete knave, and the

woman hath found him already.   270

RODERIGO I cannot believe that in her. She's full of

most blessed condition.

IAGO Blessed fig's end! The wine she drinks is made of

grapes. If she had been blessed, she would never

have loved the Moor. Blessed pudding! Didst thou   275

not see her paddle with the palm of his hand? Didst

not mark that?

RODERIGO Yes, that I did. But that was but courtesy.

IAGO Lechery, by this hand! An index and obscure

prologue to the history of lust and foul thoughts.   280

They met so near with their lips that their breaths

NOTES

61

embraced together. Villainous thoughts, Roderigo!
When these mutualities so marshal the way, hard
at hand comes the master and main exercise, th'
incorporate conclusion. Pish! But, sir, be you ruled   285
by me. I have brought you from Venice. Watch you
tonight. For the command, I'll lay 't upon you.
Cassio knows you not. I'll not be far from you. Do
you find some occasion to anger Cassio, either by
speaking too loud, or tainting his discipline, or from   290
what other course you please, which the time shall
more favorably minister.

RODERIGO Well.

IAGO Sir, he's rash and very sudden in choler, and
haply may strike at you. Provoke him that he may,   295
for even out of that will I cause these of Cyprus to
mutiny, whose qualification shall come into no
true taste again but by the displanting of Cassio. So
shall you have a shorter journey to your desires by
the means I shall then have to prefer them, and the   300
impediment most profitably removed, without the
which there were no expectation of our prosperity.

NOTES

RODERIGO I will do this, if you can bring it to any

    opportunity.

IAGO I warrant thee. Meet me by and by at the citadel. I   305

    must fetch his necessaries ashore. Farewell.

RODERIGO Adieu.   *He exits.*

IAGO

    That Cassio loves her, I do well believe 't.

    That she loves him, 'tis apt and of great credit.

    The Moor, howbeit that I endure him not,   310

    Is of a constant, loving, noble nature,

    And I dare think he'll prove to Desdemona

    A most dear husband. Now, I do love her too,

    Not out of absolute lust (though peradventure

    I stand accountant for as great a sin)   315

    But partly led to diet my revenge

    For that I do suspect the lusty Moor

    Hath leaped into my seat—the thought whereof

    Doth, like a poisonous mineral, gnaw my inwards,

    And nothing can or shall content my soul   320

    Till I am evened with him, wife for wife,

    Or, failing so, yet that I put the Moor

    At least into a jealousy so strong

NOTES

That judgment cannot cure. Which thing to do,

If this poor trash of Venice, whom I trace   325

For his quick hunting, stand the putting on,

I'll have our Michael Cassio on the hip,

Abuse him to the Moor in the rank garb

(For I fear Cassio with my nightcap too),

Make the Moor thank me, love me, and reward me   330

For making him egregiously an ass

And practicing upon his peace and quiet

Even to madness. 'Tis here, but yet confused.

Knavery's plain face is never seen till used.

He exits.

NOTES

Scene 2

Enter Othello's Herald with a proclamation.

HERALD It is Othello's pleasure, our noble and valiant

    general, that upon certain tidings now arrived,

    importing the mere perdition of the Turkish fleet,

    every man put himself into triumph: some to

    dance, some to make bonfires, each man to what   5

    sport and revels his addition leads him. For besides

    these beneficial news, it is the celebration of his

    nuptial. So much was his pleasure should be proclaimed

    All offices are open, and there is full

    liberty of feasting from this present hour of five till   10

    the bell have told eleven. Heaven bless the isle of

    Cyprus and our noble general, Othello!

He exits.

NOTES

Scene 3

Enter Othello, Desdemona, Cassio, and Attendants.

OTHELLO

  Good Michael, look you to the guard tonight.

  Let's teach ourselves that honorable stop

  Not to outsport discretion.

CASSIO

  Iago hath direction what to do,

  But notwithstanding, with my personal eye   5

  Will I look to 't.

OTHELLO Iago is most honest.

  Michael, goodnight. Tomorrow with your earliest

  Let me have speech with you. *To Desdemona.* Come,

    my dear love,   10

  The purchase made, the fruits are to ensue;

  That profit's yet to come 'tween me and you.—

  Goodnight.

Othello and Desdemona exit, with Attendants.

Enter Iago.

NOTES

CASSIO

  Welcome, Iago. We must to the watch.

IAGO Not this hour, lieutenant. 'Tis not yet ten o' th'   15

  clock. Our general cast us thus early for the love of

  his Desdemona—who let us not therefore blame;

  he hath not yet made wanton the night with her, and

  she is sport for Jove.

CASSIO She's a most exquisite lady.   20

IAGO And, I'll warrant her, full of game.

CASSIO Indeed, she's a most fresh and delicate

  creature.

IAGO What an eye she has! Methinks it sounds a parley

  to provocation.   25

CASSIO An inviting eye, and yet methinks right

  modest.

IAGO And when she speaks, is it not an alarum to love?

CASSIO She is indeed perfection.

IAGO Well, happiness to their sheets! Come, lieutenant,   30

  I have a stoup of wine; and here without are a

  brace of Cyprus gallants that would fain have a

  measure to the health of black Othello.

CASSIO Not tonight, good Iago. I have very poor and

NOTES

unhappy brains for drinking. I could well wish 35

    courtesy would invent some other custom of

    entertainment.

IAGO O, they are our friends! But one cup; I'll drink

    for you.

CASSIO I have drunk but one cup tonight, and that was 40

    craftily qualified too, and behold what innovation it

    makes here. I am unfortunate in the infirmity and

    dare not task my weakness with any more.

IAGO What, man! 'Tis a night of revels. The gallants

    desire it. 45

CASSIO Where are they?

IAGO Here at the door. I pray you, call them in.

CASSIO I'll do 't, but it dislikes me. *He exits.*

IAGO

    If I can fasten but one cup upon him

    With that which he hath drunk tonight already, 50

    He'll be as full of quarrel and offense

    As my young mistress' dog. Now my sick fool

      Roderigo,

    Whom love hath turned almost the wrong side out,

    To Desdemona hath tonight caroused 55

NOTES

Potations pottle-deep; and he's to watch.

Three else of Cyprus, noble swelling spirits

That hold their honors in a wary distance,

The very elements of this warlike isle,

Have I tonight flustered with flowing cups;   60

And they watch too. Now, 'mongst this flock of

  drunkards

Am I to put our Cassio in some action

That may offend the isle. But here they come.

If consequence do but approve my dream,   65

My boat sails freely both with wind and stream.

Enter Cassio, Montano, and Gentlemen, followed by

Servants with wine.

CASSIO 'Fore God, they have given me a rouse

  already.

MONTANO Good faith, a little one; not past a pint, as I

  am a soldier.   70

IAGO Some wine, ho!

  Sings. And let me the cannikin clink, clink,

    And let me the cannikin clink.

NOTES

A soldier's a man,

O, man's life's but a span,   75

Why, then, let a soldier drink.

Some wine, boys!

CASSIO 'Fore God, an excellent song.

IAGO I learned it in England, where indeed they are

most potent in potting. Your Dane, your German,   80

and your swag-bellied Hollander—drink, ho!—are

nothing to your English.

CASSIO Is your Englishman so exquisite in his

drinking?

IAGO Why, he drinks you, with facility, your Dane   85

dead drunk. He sweats not to overthrow your Almain.

He gives your Hollander a vomit ere the next

pottle can be filled.

CASSIO To the health of our general!

MONTANO I am for it, lieutenant, and I'll do you   90

justice.

IAGO O sweet England!

Sings. King Stephen was and-a worthy peer,

His breeches cost him but a crown;

He held them sixpence all too dear;   95

NOTES

With that he called the tailor lown.

He was a wight of high renown,

And thou art but of low degree;

'Tis pride that pulls the country down,

Then take thy auld cloak about thee. 100

Some wine, ho!

CASSIO 'Fore God, this is a more exquisite song than

the other!

IAGO Will you hear 't again?

CASSIO No, for I hold him to be unworthy of his place 105

that does those things. Well, God's above all; and

there be souls must be saved, and there be souls

must not be saved.

IAGO It's true, good lieutenant.

CASSIO For mine own part—no offense to the General, 110

nor any man of quality—I hope to be saved.

IAGO And so do I too, lieutenant.

CASSIO Ay, but, by your leave, not before me. The

Lieutenant is to be saved before the Ancient. Let's

have no more of this. Let's to our affairs. God 115

forgive us our sins! Gentlemen, let's look to our

business. Do not think, gentlemen, I am drunk. This

NOTES

is my ancient, this is my right hand, and this is my

left. I am not drunk now. I can stand well enough,

and I speak well enough. 120

GENTLEMEN Excellent well.

CASSIO Why, very well then. You must not think then

that I am drunk. *He exits.*

MONTANO

To th' platform, masters. Come, let's set the watch.

Gentlemen exit.

IAGO, *to Montano*

You see this fellow that is gone before? 125

He's a soldier fit to stand by Caesar

And give direction; and do but see his vice.

'Tis to his virtue a just equinox,

The one as long as th' other. 'Tis pity of him.

I fear the trust Othello puts him in, 130

On some odd time of his infirmity,

Will shake this island.

MONTANO But is he often thus?

IAGO

'Tis evermore the prologue to his sleep.

He'll watch the horologe a double set 135

NOTES

If drink rock not his cradle.

MONTANO It were well

    The General were put in mind of it.

    Perhaps he sees it not, or his good nature

    Prizes the virtue that appears in Cassio   140

    And looks not on his evils. Is not this true?

Enter Roderigo.

IAGO*, aside to Roderigo* How now, Roderigo?

    I pray you, after the Lieutenant, go.

Roderigo exits.

MONTANO

    And 'tis great pity that the noble Moor

    Should hazard such a place as his own second   145

    With one of an engraffed infirmity.

    It were an honest action to say so

    To the Moor.

IAGO Not I, for this fair island.

    I do love Cassio well and would do much   150

    To cure him of this evil— "   *Help, help!" within.*

     But hark! What noise?

NOTES

Enter Cassio, pursuing Roderigo.

CASSIO Zounds, you rogue, you rascal!

MONTANO What's the matter, lieutenant?

CASSIO A knave teach me my duty? I'll beat the knave   155

    into a twiggen bottle.

RODERIGO Beat me?

CASSIO Dost thou prate, rogue?   *He hits Roderigo.*

MONTANO Nay, good lieutenant. I pray you, sir, hold

    your hand.   160

CASSIO Let me go, sir, or I'll knock you o'er the

    mazard.

MONTANO Come, come, you're drunk.

CASSIO Drunk?

They fight.

IAGO*, aside to Roderigo*

    Away, I say! Go out and cry a mutiny.   165

Roderigo exits.

    Nay, good lieutenant.—God's will, gentlemen!—

    Help, ho! Lieutenant—sir—Montano—sir—

    Help, masters!—Here's a goodly watch indeed!

NOTES

Who's that which rings the bell? Diablo, ho!

The town will rise. God's will, lieutenant, hold!   170

You will be shamed forever.

Enter Othello and Attendants.

OTHELLO

What is the matter here?

MONTANO Zounds, I bleed

still.

I am hurt to th' death. He dies!   *He attacks Cassio.* 175

OTHELLO Hold, for your lives!

IAGO

Hold, ho! Lieutenant—sir—Montano—

gentlemen—

Have you forgot all sense of place and duty?

Hold! The General speaks to you. Hold, for shame!   180

OTHELLO

Why, how now, ho! From whence ariseth this?

Are we turned Turks, and to ourselves do that

Which heaven hath forbid the Ottomites?

NOTES

For Christian shame, put by this barbarous brawl!

He that stirs next to carve for his own rage   185

Holds his soul light; he dies upon his motion.

Silence that dreadful bell. It frights the isle

From her propriety. What is the matter, masters?

Honest Iago, that looks dead with grieving,

Speak. Who began this? On thy love, I charge thee.   190

IAGO

I do not know. Friends all but now, even now,

In quarter and in terms like bride and groom

Divesting them for bed; and then but now,

As if some planet had unwitted men,

Swords out, and tilting one at other's breast,   195

In opposition bloody. I cannot speak

Any beginning to this peevish odds,

And would in action glorious I had lost

Those legs that brought me to a part of it!

OTHELLO

How comes it, Michael, you are thus forgot?   200

CASSIO

I pray you pardon me; I cannot speak.

NOTES

OTHELLO

 Worthy Montano, you were wont be civil.

 The gravity and stillness of your youth

 The world hath noted. And your name is great

 In mouths of wisest censure. What's the matter   205

 That you unlace your reputation thus,

 And spend your rich opinion for the name

 Of a night-brawler? Give me answer to it.

MONTANO

 Worthy Othello, I am hurt to danger.

 Your officer Iago can inform you,   210

 While I spare speech, which something now offends

     me,

 Of all that I do know; nor know I aught

 By me that's said or done amiss this night,

 Unless self-charity be sometimes a vice,   215

 And to defend ourselves it be a sin

 When violence assails us.

OTHELLO Now, by heaven,

 My blood begins my safer guides to rule,

 And passion, having my best judgment collied,   220

 Assays to lead the way. Zounds, if I stir,

NOTES

Or do but lift this arm, the best of you

Shall sink in my rebuke. Give me to know

How this foul rout began, who set it on;

And he that is approved in this offense,   225

Though he had twinned with me, both at a birth,

Shall lose me. What, in a town of war

Yet wild, the people's hearts brimful of fear,

To manage private and domestic quarrel,

In night, and on the court and guard of safety?   230

'Tis monstrous. Iago, who began 't?

MONTANO

If partially affined, or leagued in office,

Thou dost deliver more or less than truth,

Thou art no soldier.

IAGO Touch me not so near.   235

I had rather have this tongue cut from my mouth

Than it should do offense to Michael Cassio.

Yet I persuade myself, to speak the truth

Shall nothing wrong him. Thus it is, general:

Montano and myself being in speech,   240

There comes a fellow crying out for help,

And Cassio following him with determined sword

NOTES

To execute upon him. Sir, this gentleman

Pointing to Montano.

Steps in to Cassio and entreats his pause.

Myself the crying fellow did pursue,   245

Lest by his clamor—as it so fell out—

The town might fall in fright. He, swift of foot,

Outran my purpose, and I returned the rather

For that I heard the clink and fall of swords

And Cassio high in oath, which till tonight   250

I ne'er might say before. When I came back—

For this was brief—I found them close together

At blow and thrust, even as again they were

When you yourself did part them.

More of this matter cannot I report.   255

But men are men; the best sometimes forget.

Though Cassio did some little wrong to him,

As men in rage strike those that wish them best,

Yet surely Cassio, I believe, received

From him that fled some strange indignity   260

Which patience could not pass.

OTHELLO I know, Iago,

Thy honesty and love doth mince this matter,

NOTES

Making it light to Cassio.—Cassio, I love thee,

But nevermore be officer of mine.   265

Enter Desdemona attended.

Look if my gentle love be not raised up!

I'll make thee an example.

DESDEMONA

What is the matter, dear?

OTHELLO All's well now,

   sweeting.   270

Come away to bed. *To Montano.* Sir, for your hurts,

Myself will be your surgeon.—Lead him off.

                                                    Montano is led off.

Iago, look with care about the town

And silence those whom this vile brawl

   distracted.—   275

Come, Desdemona. 'Tis the soldier's life

To have their balmy slumbers waked with strife.

                                           All but Iago and Cassio exit.

IAGO What, are you hurt, lieutenant?

CASSIO Ay, past all surgery.

NOTES

IAGO Marry, God forbid!   280

CASSIO Reputation, reputation, reputation! O, I have

lost my reputation! I have lost the immortal part of

myself, and what remains is bestial. My reputation,

Iago, my reputation!

IAGO As I am an honest man, I thought you had   285

received some bodily wound. There is more sense

in that than in reputation. Reputation is an idle and

most false imposition, oft got without merit and lost

without deserving. You have lost no reputation at

all, unless you repute yourself such a loser. What,   290

man, there are ways to recover the General again!

You are but now cast in his mood—a punishment

more in policy than in malice, even so as one would

beat his offenseless dog to affright an imperious

lion. Sue to him again and he's yours.   295

CASSIO I will rather sue to be despised than to deceive

so good a commander with so slight, so drunken,

and so indiscreet an officer. Drunk? And speak

parrot? And squabble? Swagger? Swear? And discourse

fustian with one's own shadow? O thou   300

invisible spirit of wine, if thou hast no name to be

NOTES

known by, let us call thee devil!

IAGO What was he that you followed with your sword?

What had he done to you?

CASSIO I know not.   305

IAGO Is 't possible?

CASSIO I remember a mass of things, but nothing

distinctly; a quarrel, but nothing wherefore. O

God, that men should put an enemy in their

mouths to steal away their brains! That we should   310

with joy, pleasance, revel, and applause transform

ourselves into beasts!

IAGO Why, but you are now well enough. How came

you thus recovered?

CASSIO It hath pleased the devil drunkenness to give   315

place to the devil wrath. One unperfectness shows

me another, to make me frankly despise myself.

IAGO Come, you are too severe a moraler. As the time,

the place, and the condition of this country stands,

I could heartily wish this had not so befallen. But   320

since it is as it is, mend it for your own good.

CASSIO I will ask him for my place again; he shall tell

me I am a drunkard! Had I as many mouths as

NOTES

82

Hydra, such an answer would stop them all. To be

now a sensible man, by and by a fool, and presently   325

a beast! O, strange! Every inordinate cup is unblessed,

and the ingredient is a devil.

IAGO Come, come, good wine is a good familiar creature,

if it be well used. Exclaim no more against it.

And, good lieutenant, I think you think I love you.   330

CASSIO I have well approved it, sir.—I drunk!

IAGO You or any man living may be drunk at a time,

man. I'll tell you what you shall do. Our general's

wife is now the general: I may say so in this

respect, for that he hath devoted and given up   335

himself to the contemplation, mark, and denotement

of her parts and graces. Confess yourself

freely to her. Importune her help to put you in your

place again. She is of so free, so kind, so apt, so

blessed a disposition she holds it a vice in her   340

goodness not to do more than she is requested. This

broken joint between you and her husband entreat

her to splinter, and, my fortunes against any lay

worth naming, this crack of your love shall grow

stronger than it was before.   345

NOTES

CASSIO You advise me well.

IAGO I protest, in the sincerity of love and honest

   kindness.

CASSIO I think it freely; and betimes in the morning I

   will beseech the virtuous Desdemona to undertake   350

   for me. I am desperate of my fortunes if they check

   me here.

IAGO You are in the right. Good night, lieutenant. I

   must to the watch.

CASSIO Good night, honest Iago.   *Cassio exits.* 355

IAGO

   And what's he, then, that says I play the villain,

   When this advice is free I give and honest,

   Probal to thinking, and indeed the course

   To win the Moor again? For 'tis most easy

   Th' inclining Desdemona to subdue   360

   In any honest suit. She's framed as fruitful

   As the free elements. And then for her

   To win the Moor—were 't to renounce his baptism,

   All seals and symbols of redeemèd sin—

   His soul is so enfettered to her love   365

   That she may make, unmake, do what she list,

NOTES

Even as her appetite shall play the god

With his weak function. How am I then a villain

To counsel Cassio to this parallel course

Directly to his good? Divinity of hell!   370

When devils will the blackest sins put on,

They do suggest at first with heavenly shows,

As I do now. For whiles this honest fool

Plies Desdemona to repair his fortune,

And she for him pleads strongly to the Moor,   375

I'll pour this pestilence into his ear:

That she repeals him for her body's lust;

And by how much she strives to do him good,

She shall undo her credit with the Moor.

So will I turn her virtue into pitch,   380

And out of her own goodness make the net

That shall enmesh them all.

Enter Roderigo.

   How now, Roderigo?

RODERIGO I do follow here in the chase, not like a

   hound that hunts, but one that fills up the cry. My   385

NOTES

money is almost spent, I have been tonight exceedingly

well cudgeled, and I think the issue will be I

shall have so much experience for my pains, and so,

with no money at all and a little more wit, return

again to Venice.   390

IAGO

How poor are they that have not patience!

What wound did ever heal but by degrees?

Thou know'st we work by wit and not by witchcraft,

And wit depends on dilatory time.

Does 't not go well? Cassio hath beaten thee,   395

And thou, by that small hurt, hast cashiered Cassio.

Though other things grow fair against the sun,

Yet fruits that blossom first will first be ripe.

Content thyself awhile. By th' Mass, 'tis morning!

Pleasure and action make the hours seem short.   400

Retire thee; go where thou art billeted.

Away, I say! Thou shalt know more hereafter.

Nay, get thee gone.   *Roderigo exits.*

Two things are to be done.

My wife must move for Cassio to her mistress.   405

I'll set her on.

NOTES

Myself the while to draw the Moor apart

And bring him jump when he may Cassio find

Soliciting his wife. Ay, that's the way.

Dull not device by coldness and delay.   410

He exits.

NOTES

ACT 3

Scene 1

Enter Cassio with Musicians.

CASSIO

Masters, play here (I will content your pains)

Something that's brief; and bid "Good morrow,

general."   *They play.*

Enter the Clown.

CLOWN Why masters, have your instruments been in

Naples, that they speak i' th' nose thus?   5

MUSICIAN How, sir, how?

CLOWN Are these, I pray you, wind instruments?

MUSICIAN Ay, marry, are they, sir.

CLOWN O, thereby hangs a tail.

MUSICIAN Whereby hangs a tale, sir?   10

CLOWN Marry, sir, by many a wind instrument that I

know. But, masters, here's money for you; and the

NOTES

General so likes your music that he desires you, for

love's sake, to make no more noise with it.

MUSICIAN Well, sir, we will not.   15

CLOWN If you have any music that may not be heard, to

't again. But, as they say, to hear music the General

does not greatly care.

MUSICIAN We have none such, sir.

CLOWN Then put up your pipes in your bag, for I'll   20

away. Go, vanish into air, away!

Musicians exit.

CASSIO Dost thou hear, mine honest friend?

CLOWN No, I hear not your honest friend. I hear you.

CASSIO Prithee, keep up thy quillets.   *Giving money.*

There's a poor piece of gold for thee. If the gentlewoman   25

that attends the General's wife be stirring,

tell her there's one Cassio entreats her a little favor

of speech. Wilt thou do this?

CLOWN She is stirring, sir. If she will stir hither, I shall

seem to notify unto her.   30

CASSIO

Do, good my friend.   *Clown exits.*

NOTES

Enter Iago.

In happy time, Iago.

IAGO You have not been abed, then?

CASSIO Why, no. The day had broke

    Before we parted. I have made bold, Iago,   35

    To send in to your wife. My suit to her

    Is that she will to virtuous Desdemona

    Procure me some access.

IAGO I'll send her to you presently,

    And I'll devise a mean to draw the Moor   40

    Out of the way, that your converse and business

    May be more free.

CASSIO

    I humbly thank you for 't. *Iago exits.* I never

      knew

    A Florentine more kind and honest.   45

Enter Emilia.

NOTES

EMILIA

    Good morrow, good lieutenant. I am sorry

    For your displeasure, but all will sure be well.

    The General and his wife are talking of it,

    And she speaks for you stoutly. The Moor replies

    That he you hurt is of great fame in Cyprus   50

    And great affinity, and that in wholesome wisdom

    He might not but refuse you. But he protests he

      loves you

    And needs no other suitor but his likings

    To take the safest occasion by the front   55

    To bring you in again.

CASSIO Yet I beseech you,

    If you think fit, or that it may be done,

    Give me advantage of some brief discourse

    With Desdemon alone.   60

EMILIA Pray you come in.

    I will bestow you where you shall have time

    To speak your bosom freely.

CASSIO I am much bound to you.

They exit.

NOTES

NOTES

Scene 2

Enter Othello, Iago, and Gentlemen.

OTHELLO

  These letters give, Iago, to the pilot

  And by him do my duties to the Senate.

He gives Iago some papers.

  That done, I will be walking on the works.

  Repair there to me.

IAGO Well, my good lord, I'll do 't.   5

OTHELLO

  This fortification, gentlemen, shall we see 't?

GENTLEMEN

  We wait upon your Lordship.

They exit.

NOTES

Scene 3

Enter Desdemona, Cassio, and Emilia.

DESDEMONA

Be thou assured, good Cassio, I will do

All my abilities in thy behalf.

EMILIA

Good madam, do. I warrant it grieves my husband

As if the cause were his.

DESDEMONA

O, that's an honest fellow! Do not doubt, Cassio,   5

But I will have my lord and you again

As friendly as you were.

CASSIO Bounteous madam,

Whatever shall become of Michael Cassio,

He's never anything but your true servant.   10

DESDEMONA

I know 't. I thank you. You do love my lord;

You have known him long; and be you well assured

He shall in strangeness stand no farther off

Than in a politic distance.

NOTES

CASSIO Ay, but, lady,   15

  That policy may either last so long,

  Or feed upon such nice and waterish diet,

  Or breed itself so out of circumstance,

  That, I being absent and my place supplied,

  My general will forget my love and service.   20

DESDEMONA

  Do not doubt that. Before Emilia here,

  I give thee warrant of thy place. Assure thee,

  If I do vow a friendship, I'll perform it

  To the last article. My lord shall never rest:

  I'll watch him tame and talk him out of patience;   25

  His bed shall seem a school, his board a shrift;

  I'll intermingle everything he does

  With Cassio's suit. Therefore be merry, Cassio,

  For thy solicitor shall rather die

  Than give thy cause away.   30

Enter Othello and Iago.

EMILIA Madam, here comes my lord.

CASSIO Madam, I'll take my leave.

NOTES

DESDEMONA Why, stay, and hear me speak.

CASSIO

   Madam, not now. I am very ill at ease,

   Unfit for mine own purposes.   35

DESDEMONA Well, do your discretion.   *Cassio exits.*

IAGO

   Ha, I like not that.

OTHELLO What dost thou say?

IAGO

   Nothing, my lord; or if—I know not what.

OTHELLO

   Was not that Cassio parted from my wife?   40

IAGO

   Cassio, my lord? No, sure, I cannot think it

   That he would steal away so guiltylike,

   Seeing your coming.

OTHELLO I do believe 'twas he.

DESDEMONA How now, my lord?   45

   I have been talking with a suitor here,

   A man that languishes in your displeasure.

OTHELLO Who is 't you mean?

NOTES

DESDEMONA

Why, your lieutenant, Cassio. Good my lord,

If I have any grace or power to move you,   50

His present reconciliation take;

For if he be not one that truly loves you,

That errs in ignorance and not in cunning,

I have no judgment in an honest face.

I prithee call him back.   55

OTHELLO Went he hence now?

DESDEMONA Yes, faith, so humbled

That he hath left part of his grief with me

To suffer with him. Good love, call him back.

OTHELLO

Not now, sweet Desdemon. Some other time.   60

DESDEMONA

But shall 't be shortly?

OTHELLO The sooner, sweet, for you.

DESDEMONA

Shall 't be tonight at supper?

OTHELLO No, not tonight.

DESDEMONA Tomorrow dinner, then?   65

OTHELLO I shall not dine at home;

NOTES

I meet the captains at the citadel.

DESDEMONA

    Why then tomorrow night, or Tuesday morn,

    On Tuesday noon or night; on Wednesday morn.

    I prithee name the time, but let it not   70

    Exceed three days. In faith, he's penitent;

    And yet his trespass, in our common reason—

    Save that, they say, the wars must make example

    Out of her best—is not almost a fault

    T' incur a private check. When shall he come?   75

    Tell me, Othello. I wonder in my soul

    What you would ask me that I should deny,

    Or stand so mamm'ring on? What? Michael Cassio,

    That came a-wooing with you, and so many a time,

    When I have spoke of you dispraisingly,   80

    Hath ta'en your part—to have so much to do

    To bring him in! By 'r Lady, I could do much—

OTHELLO

    Prithee, no more. Let him come when he will;

    I will deny thee nothing.

DESDEMONA Why, this is not a boon!   85

    'Tis as I should entreat you wear your gloves,

NOTES

Or feed on nourishing dishes, or keep you warm,

Or sue to you to do a peculiar profit

To your own person. Nay, when I have a suit

Wherein I mean to touch your love indeed,   90

It shall be full of poise and difficult weight,

And fearful to be granted.

OTHELLO I will deny thee nothing!

Whereon, I do beseech thee, grant me this,

To leave me but a little to myself.   95

DESDEMONA

Shall I deny you? No. Farewell, my lord.

OTHELLO

Farewell, my Desdemona. I'll come to thee straight.

DESDEMONA

Emilia, come.—Be as your fancies teach you.

Whate'er you be, I am obedient.

Desdemona and Emilia exit.

OTHELLO

Excellent wretch! Perdition catch my soul   100

But I do love thee! And when I love thee not,

Chaos is come again.

NOTES

IAGO My noble lord—

OTHELLO

What dost thou say, Iago?

IAGO Did Michael Cassio,   105

When you wooed my lady, know of your love?

OTHELLO

He did, from first to last. Why dost thou ask?

IAGO

But for a satisfaction of my thought,

No further harm.

OTHELLO Why of thy thought, Iago?   110

IAGO

I did not think he had been acquainted with her.

OTHELLO

O yes, and went between us very oft.

IAGO Indeed?

OTHELLO

Indeed? Ay, indeed! Discern'st thou aught in that?

Is he not honest?   115

IAGO Honest, my lord?

OTHELLO Honest—ay, honest.

NOTES

IAGO

  My lord, for aught I know.

OTHELLO What dost thou think?

IAGO Think, my lord?   120

OTHELLO

  "Think, my lord?" By heaven, thou echo'st me

  As if there were some monster in thy thought

  Too hideous to be shown. Thou dost mean

    something.

  I heard thee say even now, thou lik'st not that,   125

  When Cassio left my wife. What didst not like?

  And when I told thee he was of my counsel

  In my whole course of wooing, thou cried'st

    "Indeed?"

  And didst contract and purse thy brow together   130

  As if thou then hadst shut up in thy brain

  Some horrible conceit. If thou dost love me,

  Show me thy thought.

IAGO My lord, you know I love you.

OTHELLO I think thou dost;   135

  And for I know thou 'rt full of love and honesty

  And weigh'st thy words before thou giv'st them

NOTES

breath,

Therefore these stops of thine fright me the more.

For such things in a false, disloyal knave   140

Are tricks of custom; but in a man that's just,

They're close dilations working from the heart

That passion cannot rule.

IAGO For Michael Cassio,

I dare be sworn I think that he is honest.   145

OTHELLO

I think so too.

IAGO Men should be what they seem;

Or those that be not, would they might seem none!

OTHELLO Certain, men should be what they seem.

IAGO

Why then, I think Cassio's an honest man.   150

OTHELLO Nay, yet there's more in this.

I prithee speak to me as to thy thinkings,

As thou dost ruminate, and give thy worst of

thoughts

The worst of words.   155

IAGO Good my lord, pardon me.

Though I am bound to every act of duty,

NOTES

102

I am not bound to that all slaves are free to.

Utter my thoughts? Why, say they are vile and

   false—   160

As where's that palace whereinto foul things

Sometimes intrude not? Who has that breast so

   pure

But some uncleanly apprehensions

Keep leets and law days and in sessions sit   165

With meditations lawful?

OTHELLO

   Thou dost conspire against thy friend, Iago,

   If thou but think'st him wronged and mak'st his ear

   A stranger to thy thoughts.

IAGO I do beseech you,   170

   Though I perchance am vicious in my guess—

   As, I confess, it is my nature's plague

   To spy into abuses, and oft my jealousy

   Shapes faults that are not—that your wisdom

   From one that so imperfectly conceits   175

   Would take no notice, nor build yourself a trouble

   Out of his scattering and unsure observance.

   It were not for your quiet nor your good,

NOTES

Nor for my manhood, honesty, and wisdom,

To let you know my thoughts. 180

OTHELLO What dost thou mean?

IAGO

Good name in man and woman, dear my lord,

Is the immediate jewel of their souls.

Who steals my purse steals trash. 'Tis something,

nothing; 185

'Twas mine, 'tis his, and has been slave to

thousands.

But he that filches from me my good name

Robs me of that which not enriches him

And makes me poor indeed. 190

OTHELLO By heaven, I'll know thy thoughts.

IAGO

You cannot, if my heart were in your hand,

Nor shall not, whilst 'tis in my custody.

OTHELLO

Ha?

IAGO O, beware, my lord, of jealousy! 195

It is the green-eyed monster which doth mock

The meat it feeds on. That cuckold lives in bliss

NOTES

Who, certain of his fate, loves not his wronger;

But O, what damnèd minutes tells he o'er

Who dotes, yet doubts; suspects, yet strongly loves!   200

OTHELLO O misery!

IAGO

Poor and content is rich, and rich enough;

But riches fineless is as poor as winter

To him that ever fears he shall be poor.

Good God, the souls of all my tribe defend   205

From jealousy!

OTHELLO Why, why is this?

Think'st thou I'd make a life of jealousy,

To follow still the changes of the moon

With fresh suspicions? No. To be once in doubt   210

Is once to be resolved. Exchange me for a goat

When I shall turn the business of my soul

To such exsufflicate and blown surmises,

Matching thy inference. 'Tis not to make me jealous

To say my wife is fair, feeds well, loves company,   215

Is free of speech, sings, plays, and dances well.

Where virtue is, these are more virtuous.

Nor from mine own weak merits will I draw

NOTES

The smallest fear or doubt of her revolt,

For she had eyes, and chose me. No, Iago,   220

I'll see before I doubt; when I doubt, prove;

And on the proof, there is no more but this:

Away at once with love or jealousy.

IAGO

I am glad of this, for now I shall have reason

To show the love and duty that I bear you   225

With franker spirit. Therefore, as I am bound,

Receive it from me. I speak not yet of proof.

Look to your wife; observe her well with Cassio;

Wear your eyes thus, not jealous nor secure.

I would not have your free and noble nature,   230

Out of self-bounty, be abused. Look to 't.

I know our country disposition well.

In Venice they do let God see the pranks

They dare not show their husbands. Their best

  conscience   235

Is not to leave 't undone, but keep 't unknown.

OTHELLO Dost thou say so?

IAGO

She did deceive her father, marrying you,

NOTES

And when she seemed to shake and fear your looks,

She loved them most.   240

OTHELLO And so she did.

IAGO Why, go to, then!

She that, so young, could give out such a seeming,

To seel her father's eyes up close as oak,

He thought 'twas witchcraft! But I am much to   245

blame.

I humbly do beseech you of your pardon

For too much loving you.

OTHELLO I am bound to thee forever.

IAGO

I see this hath a little dashed your spirits.   250

OTHELLO

Not a jot, not a jot.

IAGO I' faith, I fear it has.

I hope you will consider what is spoke

Comes from my love. But I do see you're moved.

I am to pray you not to strain my speech   255

To grosser issues nor to larger reach

Than to suspicion.

OTHELLO I will not.

NOTES

IAGO Should you do so, my lord,

    My speech should fall into such vile success   260

    As my thoughts aim not at. Cassio's my worthy

      friend.

    My lord, I see you're moved.

OTHELLO No, not much moved.

    I do not think but Desdemona's honest.   265

IAGO

    Long live she so! And long live you to think so!

OTHELLO

    And yet, how nature erring from itself—

IAGO

    Ay, there's the point. As, to be bold with you,

    Not to affect many proposèd matches

    Of her own clime, complexion, and degree,   270

    Whereto we see in all things nature tends—

    Foh! One may smell in such a will most rank,

    Foul disproportion, thoughts unnatural—

    But pardon me—I do not in position

    Distinctly speak of her, though I may fear   275

    Her will, recoiling to her better judgment,

    May fall to match you with her country forms

NOTES

And happily repent.

OTHELLO Farewell, farewell!

If more thou dost perceive, let me know more.   280

Set on thy wife to observe. Leave me, Iago.

IAGO, *beginning to exit* My lord, I take my leave.

OTHELLO

Why did I marry? This honest creature doubtless

Sees and knows more, much more, than he unfolds.

IAGO, *returning*

My lord, I would I might entreat your Honor   285

To scan this thing no farther. Leave it to time.

Although 'tis fit that Cassio have his place—

For sure he fills it up with great ability—

Yet, if you please to hold him off awhile,

You shall by that perceive him and his means.   290

Note if your lady strain his entertainment

With any strong or vehement importunity.

Much will be seen in that. In the meantime,

Let me be thought too busy in my fears—

As worthy cause I have to fear I am—   295

And hold her free, I do beseech your Honor.

OTHELLO Fear not my government.

NOTES

IAGO I once more take my leave.   *He exits.*

OTHELLO

This fellow's of exceeding honesty,

And knows all qualities with a learnèd spirit   300

Of human dealings. If I do prove her haggard,

Though that her jesses were my dear heartstrings,

I'd whistle her off and let her down the wind

To prey at fortune. Haply, for I am black

And have not those soft parts of conversation   305

That chamberers have, or for I am declined

Into the vale of years—yet that's not much—

She's gone, I am abused, and my relief

Must be to loathe her. O curse of marriage,

That we can call these delicate creatures ours   310

And not their appetites! I had rather be a toad

And live upon the vapor of a dungeon

Than keep a corner in the thing I love

For others' uses. Yet 'tis the plague of great ones;

Prerogatived are they less than the base.   315

'Tis destiny unshunnable, like death.

Even then this forkèd plague is fated to us

When we do quicken. Look where she comes.

NOTES

If she be false, heaven mocks itself!

I'll not believe 't.   320

DESDEMONA How now, my dear Othello?

Your dinner, and the generous islanders

By you invited, do attend your presence.

OTHELLO I am to blame.

DESDEMONA

Why do you speak so faintly? Are you not well?   325

OTHELLO

I have a pain upon my forehead, here.

DESDEMONA

Faith, that's with watching. 'Twill away again.

Let me but bind it hard; within this hour

It will be well.

OTHELLO Your napkin is too little.   330

Let it alone.   *The handkerchief falls, unnoticed.*

Come, I'll go in with you.

DESDEMONA

I am very sorry that you are not well.

NOTES

EMILIA, *picking up the handkerchief*

I am glad I have found this napkin.

This was her first remembrance from the Moor.   335

My wayward husband hath a hundred times

Wooed me to steal it. But she so loves the token

(For he conjured her she should ever keep it)

That she reserves it evermore about her

To kiss and talk to. I'll have the work ta'en out   340

And give 't Iago. What he will do with it

Heaven knows, not I.

I nothing but to please his fantasy.

Enter Iago.

IAGO How now? What do you here alone?

EMILIA

Do not you chide. I have a thing for you.   345

IAGO

You have a thing for me? It is a common thing—

EMILIA Ha?

IAGO To have a foolish wife.

NOTES

EMILIA

    O, is that all? What will you give me now

    For that same handkerchief?   350

IAGO What handkerchief?

EMILIA What handkerchief?

    Why, that the Moor first gave to Desdemona,

    That which so often you did bid me steal.

IAGO Hast stol'n it from her?   355

EMILIA

    No, faith, she let it drop by negligence,

    And to th' advantage I, being here, took 't up.

    Look, here 'tis.

IAGO A good wench! Give it me.

EMILIA

    What will you do with 't, that you have been so   360

      earnest

    To have me filch it?

IAGO*, snatching it* Why, what is that to you?

EMILIA

    If it be not for some purpose of import,

    Give 't me again. Poor lady, she'll run mad   365

    When she shall lack it.

NOTES

IAGO Be not acknown on 't.

I have use for it. Go, leave me.   *Emilia exits.*

I will in Cassio's lodging lose this napkin

And let him find it. Trifles light as air   370

Are to the jealous confirmations strong

As proofs of holy writ. This may do something.

The Moor already changes with my poison;

Dangerous conceits are in their natures poisons,

Which at the first are scarce found to distaste,   375

But with a little act upon the blood

Burn like the mines of sulfur.

Enter Othello.

  I did say so.

Look where he comes. Not poppy nor mandragora

Nor all the drowsy syrups of the world   380

Shall ever medicine thee to that sweet sleep

Which thou owedst yesterday.

OTHELLO Ha, ha, false to me?

IAGO

Why, how now, general? No more of that!

NOTES

OTHELLO

    Avaunt! Begone! Thou hast set me on the rack.   385

    I swear 'tis better to be much abused

    Than but to know 't a little.

IAGO How now, my lord?

OTHELLO

    What sense had I of her stol'n hours of lust?

    I saw 't not, thought it not; it harmed not me.   390

    I slept the next night well, fed well, was free and

      merry.

    I found not Cassio's kisses on her lips.

    He that is robbed, not wanting what is stol'n,

    Let him not know 't, and he's not robbed at all.   395

IAGO I am sorry to hear this.

OTHELLO

    I had been happy if the general camp,

    Pioners and all, had tasted her sweet body,

    So I had nothing known. O, now, forever

    Farewell the tranquil mind! Farewell content!   400

    Farewell the plumèd troops and the big wars

    That makes ambition virtue! O, farewell!

    Farewell the neighing steed and the shrill trump,

NOTES

The spirit-stirring drum, th' ear-piercing fife,

The royal banner, and all quality, 405

Pride, pomp, and circumstance of glorious war!

And O you mortal engines, whose rude throats

Th' immortal Jove's dread clamors counterfeit,

Farewell! Othello's occupation's gone!

IAGO Is 't possible, my lord? 410

OTHELLO

Villain, be sure thou prove my love a whore!

Be sure of it. Give me the ocular proof,

Or, by the worth of mine eternal soul,

Thou hadst been better have been born a dog

Than answer my waked wrath. 415

IAGO Is 't come to this?

OTHELLO

Make me to see 't, or at the least so prove it

That the probation bear no hinge nor loop

To hang a doubt on, or woe upon thy life!

IAGO My noble lord— 420

OTHELLO

If thou dost slander her and torture me,

Never pray more. Abandon all remorse;

NOTES

On horror's head horrors accumulate;

Do deeds to make heaven weep, all Earth amazed;

For nothing canst thou to damnation add   425

Greater than that.

IAGO O grace! O heaven forgive me!

Are you a man? Have you a soul or sense?

God b' wi' you. Take mine office.—O wretched fool,

That liv'st to make thine honesty a vice!—   430

O monstrous world! Take note, take note, O world:

To be direct and honest is not safe.—

I thank you for this profit, and from hence

I'll love no friend, sith love breeds such offense.

OTHELLO Nay, stay. Thou shouldst be honest.   435

IAGO

I should be wise; for honesty's a fool

And loses that it works for.

OTHELLO By the world,

I think my wife be honest and think she is not.

I think that thou art just and think thou art not.   440

I'll have some proof! Her name, that was as fresh

As Dian's visage, is now begrimed and black

As mine own face. If there be cords, or knives,

NOTES

Poison, or fire, or suffocating streams,

I'll not endure it. Would I were satisfied!   445

IAGO

I see you are eaten up with passion.

I do repent me that I put it to you.

You would be satisfied?

OTHELLO Would? Nay, and I will.

IAGO

And may; but how? How satisfied, my lord?   450

Would you, the supervisor, grossly gape on,

Behold her topped?

OTHELLO Death and damnation! O!

IAGO

It were a tedious difficulty, I think,

To bring them to that prospect. Damn them then   455

If ever mortal eyes do see them bolster

More than their own! What then? How then?

What shall I say? Where's satisfaction?

It is impossible you should see this,

Were they as prime as goats, as hot as monkeys,   460

As salt as wolves in pride, and fools as gross

As ignorance made drunk. But yet I say,

NOTES

If imputation and strong circumstances

Which lead directly to the door of truth

Will give you satisfaction, you might have 't.   465

OTHELLO

Give me a living reason she's disloyal.

IAGO I do not like the office,

But sith I am entered in this cause so far,

Pricked to 't by foolish honesty and love,

I will go on. I lay with Cassio lately,   470

And being troubled with a raging tooth

I could not sleep. There are a kind of men

So loose of soul that in their sleeps will mutter

Their affairs. One of this kind is Cassio.

In sleep I heard him say "Sweet Desdemona,   475

Let us be wary, let us hide our loves."

And then, sir, would he gripe and wring my hand,

Cry "O sweet creature!" then kiss me hard,

As if he plucked up kisses by the roots

That grew upon my lips; then laid his leg   480

O'er my thigh, and sighed, and kissed, and then

Cried "Cursèd fate that gave thee to the Moor!"

NOTES

OTHELLO

O monstrous! Monstrous!

IAGO Nay, this was but his

dream.   485

OTHELLO

But this denoted a foregone conclusion.

'Tis a shrewd doubt, though it be but a dream.

IAGO

And this may help to thicken other proofs

That do demonstrate thinly.

OTHELLO I'll tear her all to pieces.   490

IAGO

Nay, but be wise. Yet we see nothing done.

She may be honest yet. Tell me but this:

Have you not sometimes seen a handkerchief

Spotted with strawberries in your wife's hand?

OTHELLO

I gave her such a one. 'Twas my first gift.   495

IAGO

I know not that; but such a handkerchief—

I am sure it was your wife's—did I today

See Cassio wipe his beard with.

NOTES

OTHELLO If it be that—

IAGO

    If it be that, or any that was hers,   500

    It speaks against her with the other proofs.

OTHELLO

    O, that the slave had forty thousand lives!

    One is too poor, too weak for my revenge.

    Now do I see 'tis true. Look here, Iago,

    All my fond love thus do I blow to heaven.   505

    'Tis gone.

    Arise, black vengeance, from the hollow hell!

    Yield up, O love, thy crown and hearted throne

    To tyrannous hate! Swell, bosom, with thy fraught,

    For 'tis of aspics' tongues!   510

IAGO Yet be content.

OTHELLO O, blood, blood, blood!

IAGO

    Patience, I say. Your mind perhaps may change.

OTHELLO

    Never, Iago. Like to the Pontic Sea,

    Whose icy current and compulsive course   515

    Ne'er feels retiring ebb, but keeps due on

NOTES

121

To the Propontic and the Hellespont,

Even so my bloody thoughts, with violent pace

Shall ne'er look back, ne'er ebb to humble love,

Till that a capable and wide revenge   520

Swallow them up. *He kneels.* Now by yond marble

  heaven,

In the due reverence of a sacred vow,

I here engage my words.

IAGO Do not rise yet.   *Iago kneels.* 525

  Witness, you ever-burning lights above,

  You elements that clip us round about,

  Witness that here Iago doth give up

  The execution of his wit, hands, heart

  To wronged Othello's service! Let him command,   530

  And to obey shall be in me remorse,

  What bloody business ever.   *They rise.*

OTHELLO I greet thy love

  Not with vain thanks but with acceptance

    bounteous,   535

  And will upon the instant put thee to 't.

  Within these three days let me hear thee say

  That Cassio's not alive.

NOTES

IAGO My friend is dead.

'Tis done at your request. But let her live.   540

OTHELLO Damn her, lewd minx! O, damn her, damn

her!

Come, go with me apart. I will withdraw

To furnish me with some swift means of death

For the fair devil. Now art thou my lieutenant.   545

IAGO I am your own forever.

They exit.

NOTES

Scene 4

Enter Desdemona, Emilia, and Clown.

DESDEMONA Do you know, sirrah, where Lieutenant

Cassio lies?

CLOWN I dare not say he lies anywhere.

DESDEMONA Why, man?

CLOWN He's a soldier, and for me to say a soldier lies,   5

'tis stabbing.

DESDEMONA Go to! Where lodges he?

CLOWN To tell you where he lodges is to tell you

where I lie.

DESDEMONA Can anything be made of this?   10

CLOWN I know not where he lodges; and for me to

devise a lodging and say he lies here, or he lies

there, were to lie in mine own throat.

DESDEMONA Can you inquire him out, and be edified

by report?   15

CLOWN I will catechize the world for him—that is,

make questions, and by them answer.

DESDEMONA Seek him, bid him come hither. Tell him I

have moved my lord on his behalf and hope all will

NOTES

be well. 20

CLOWN To do this is within the compass of man's wit,

and therefore I will attempt the doing it.

Clown exits.

DESDEMONA

Where should I lose that handkerchief, Emilia?

EMILIA I know not, madam.

DESDEMONA

Believe me, I had rather have lost my purse 25

Full of crusadoes. And but my noble Moor

Is true of mind and made of no such baseness

As jealous creatures are, it were enough

To put him to ill thinking.

EMILIA Is he not jealous? 30

DESDEMONA

Who, he? I think the sun where he was born

Drew all such humors from him.

EMILIA Look where he

comes.

Enter Othello.

NOTES

DESDEMONA

I will not leave him now till Cassio   35

Be called to him.—How is 't with you, my lord?

OTHELLO

Well, my good lady. *Aside.* O, hardness to

dissemble!—

How do you, Desdemona?

DESDEMONA Well, my good lord.   40

OTHELLO

Give me your hand. *He takes her hand.* This hand

is moist, my lady.

DESDEMONA

It yet has felt no age nor known no sorrow.

OTHELLO

This argues fruitfulness and liberal heart.

Hot, hot, and moist. This hand of yours requires   45

A sequester from liberty, fasting and prayer,

Much castigation, exercise devout;

For here's a young and sweating devil here

That commonly rebels. 'Tis a good hand,

A frank one.   50

DESDEMONA You may indeed say so,

NOTES

For 'twas that hand that gave away my heart.

OTHELLO

A liberal hand! The hearts of old gave hands,

But our new heraldry is hands, not hearts.

DESDEMONA

I cannot speak of this. Come now, your promise.   55

OTHELLO What promise, chuck?

DESDEMONA

I have sent to bid Cassio come speak with you.

OTHELLO

I have a salt and sorry rheum offends me.

Lend me thy handkerchief.

DESDEMONA Here, my lord.   60

OTHELLO

That which I gave you.

DESDEMONA I have it not about me.

OTHELLO Not?

DESDEMONA No, faith, my lord.

OTHELLO That's a fault. That handkerchief   65

Did an Egyptian to my mother give.

She was a charmer, and could almost read

The thoughts of people. She told her, while she kept

NOTES

it,

’Twould make her amiable and subdue my father   70

Entirely to her love. But if she lost it,

Or made a gift of it, my father’s eye

Should hold her loathèd, and his spirits should hunt

After new fancies. She, dying, gave it me,

And bid me, when my fate would have me wived,   75

To give it her. I did so; and take heed on ’t,

Make it a darling like your precious eye.

To lose ’t or give ’t away were such perdition

As nothing else could match.

DESDEMONA Is ’t possible?   80

OTHELLO

’Tis true. There’s magic in the web of it.

A sybil that had numbered in the world

The sun to course two hundred compasses,

In her prophetic fury sewed the work.

The worms were hallowed that did breed the silk,   85

And it was dyed in mummy, which the skillful

Conserved of maidens’ hearts.

DESDEMONA I’ faith, is ’t true?

NOTES

OTHELLO

Most veritable. Therefore, look to 't well.

DESDEMONA

Then would to God that I had never seen 't!   90

OTHELLO Ha? Wherefore?

DESDEMONA

Why do you speak so startingly and rash?

OTHELLO

Is 't lost? Is 't gone? Speak, is 't out o' th' way?

DESDEMONA Heaven bless us!

OTHELLO Say you?   95

DESDEMONA

It is not lost, but what an if it were?

OTHELLO How?

DESDEMONA I say it is not lost.

OTHELLO Fetch 't. Let me see 't!

DESDEMONA

Why, so I can. But I will not now.   100

This is a trick to put me from my suit.

Pray you, let Cassio be received again.

OTHELLO

Fetch me the handkerchief! *Aside.* My mind

NOTES

misgives.

DESDEMONA Come, come.   105

You'll never meet a more sufficient man.

OTHELLO

The handkerchief!

DESDEMONA I pray, talk me of Cassio.

OTHELLOThe handkerchief!

DESDEMONA A man that all his time   110

Hath founded his good fortunes on your love;

Shared dangers with you—

OTHELLO

The handkerchief!

DESDEMONA I' faith, you are to blame.

OTHELLO Zounds!   *Othello exits.* 115

EMILIA Is not this man jealous?

DESDEMONA I ne'er saw this before.

Sure, there's some wonder in this handkerchief!

I am most unhappy in the loss of it.

EMILIA

'Tis not a year or two shows us a man.   120

They are all but stomachs, and we all but food;

They eat us hungerly, and when they are full

NOTES

They belch us.

Enter Iago and Cassio.

Look you—Cassio and my husband.

IAGO, *to Cassio*

There is no other way; 'tis she must do 't,   125

And, lo, the happiness! Go and importune her.

DESDEMONA

How now, good Cassio, what's the news with you?

CASSIO

Madam, my former suit. I do beseech you

That by your virtuous means I may again

Exist, and be a member of his love   130

Whom I with all the office of my heart

Entirely honor. I would not be delayed.

If my offense be of such mortal kind

That nor my service past nor present sorrows

Nor purposed merit in futurity   135

Can ransom me into his love again,

But to know so must be my benefit.

So shall I clothe me in a forced content,

NOTES

And shut myself up in some other course

To fortune's alms.   140

DESDEMONA Alas, thrice-gentle Cassio,

My advocation is not now in tune.

My lord is not my lord; nor should I know him

Were he in favor as in humor altered.

So help me every spirit sanctified   145

As I have spoken for you all my best,

And stood within the blank of his displeasure

For my free speech! You must awhile be patient.

What I can do I will; and more I will

Than for myself I dare. Let that suffice you.   150

IAGO

Is my lord angry?

EMILIA He went hence but now,

And certainly in strange unquietness.

IAGO

Can he be angry? I have seen the cannon

When it hath blown his ranks into the air   155

And, like the devil, from his very arm

Puffed his own brother—and is he angry?

Something of moment then. I will go meet him.

NOTES

There's matter in 't indeed if he be angry.

DESDEMONA

I prithee do so.   *He exits.* 160

  Something, sure, of state,

Either from Venice, or some unhatched practice

Made demonstrable here in Cyprus to him,

Hath puddled his clear spirit; and in such cases

Men's natures wrangle with inferior things,   165

Though great ones are their object. 'Tis even so.

For let our finger ache, and it endues

Our other healthful members even to a sense

Of pain. Nay, we must think men are not gods,

Nor of them look for such observancy   170

As fits the bridal. Beshrew me much, Emilia,

I was—unhandsome warrior as I am!—

Arraigning his unkindness with my soul.

But now I find I had suborned the witness,

And he's indicted falsely.   175

EMILIA Pray heaven it be

State matters, as you think, and no conception

Nor no jealous toy concerning you.

NOTES

DESDEMONA

Alas the day, I never gave him cause!

EMILIA

But jealous souls will not be answered so.   180

They are not ever jealous for the cause,

But jealous for they're jealous. It is a monster

Begot upon itself, born on itself.

DESDEMONA

Heaven keep that monster from Othello's mind!

EMILIA Lady, amen.   185

DESDEMONA

I will go seek him.—Cassio, walk hereabout.

If I do find him fit, I'll move your suit

And seek to effect it to my uttermost.

CASSIO I humbly thank your Ladyship.

Desdemona and Emilia exit.

Enter Bianca.

BIANCA

'Save you, friend Cassio!   190

CASSIO What make you from

NOTES

home?

How is 't with you, my most fair Bianca?

I' faith, sweet love, I was coming to your house.

BIANCA

And I was going to your lodging, Cassio.   195

What, keep a week away? Seven days and nights,

Eightscore eight hours, and lovers' absent hours

More tedious than the dial eightscore times?

O weary reck'ning!

CASSIO Pardon me, Bianca.   200

I have this while with leaden thoughts been pressed,

But I shall in a more continuate time

Strike off this score of absence. Sweet Bianca,

Giving her Desdemona's handkerchief.

Take me this work out.

BIANCA O, Cassio, whence came this?   205

This is some token from a newer friend.

To the felt absence now I feel a cause.

Is 't come to this? Well, well.

CASSIO Go to, woman!

Throw your vile guesses in the devil's teeth,   210

From whence you have them. You are jealous now

NOTES

That this is from some mistress, some

   remembrance.

   No, by my faith, Bianca.

BIANCA Why, whose is it?   215

CASSIO

   I know not neither. I found it in my chamber.

   I like the work well. Ere it be demanded,

   As like enough it will, I would have it copied.

   Take it, and do 't, and leave me for this time.

BIANCA Leave you? Wherefore?   220

CASSIO

   I do attend here on the General,

   And think it no addition, nor my wish,

   To have him see me womaned.

BIANCA Why, I pray you?

CASSIO Not that I love you not.   225

BIANCA But that you do not love me!

   I pray you bring me on the way a little,

   And say if I shall see you soon at night.

CASSIO

   'Tis but a little way that I can bring you,

   For I attend here. But I'll see you soon.   230

NOTES

BIANCA

'Tis very good. I must be circumstanced.

They exit.

NOTES

ACT 4

Scene 1

Enter Othello and Iago.

IAGO

  Will you think so?

OTHELLO Think so, Iago?

IAGO What,

  To kiss in private?

OTHELLO An unauthorized kiss!   5

IAGO

  Or to be naked with her friend in bed

  An hour or more, not meaning any harm?

OTHELLO

  Naked in bed, Iago, and not mean harm?

  It is hypocrisy against the devil!

  They that mean virtuously, and yet do so,   10

  The devil their virtue tempts, and they tempt

    heaven.

NOTES

IAGO

If they do nothing, 'tis a venial slip.

But if I give my wife a handkerchief—

OTHELLO What then?   15

IAGO

Why then, 'tis hers, my lord, and being hers,

She may, I think, bestow 't on any man.

OTHELLO

She is protectress of her honor, too.

May she give that?

IAGO

Her honor is an essence that's not seen;   20

They have it very oft that have it not.

But for the handkerchief—

OTHELLO

By heaven, I would most gladly have forgot it.

Thou saidst—O, it comes o'er my memory

As doth the raven o'er the infectious house,   25

Boding to all—he had my handkerchief.

IAGO

Ay, what of that?

OTHELLO That's not so good now.

NOTES

IAGO What

    If I had said I had seen him do you wrong?   30

    Or heard him say (as knaves be such abroad,

    Who having, by their own importunate suit

    Or voluntary dotage of some mistress,

    Convincèd or supplied them, cannot choose

    But they must blab)—   35

OTHELLO Hath he said anything?

IAGO

    He hath, my lord, but be you well assured,

    No more than he'll unswear.

OTHELLO What hath he said?

IAGO

    Faith, that he did—I know not what he did.   40

OTHELLO What? What?

IAGO

    Lie—

OTHELLO With her?

IAGO With her—on her—what you will.

OTHELLO Lie with her? Lie on her? We say "lie on her"   45

    when they belie her. Lie with her—Zounds, that's

    fulsome! Handkerchief—confessions—handkerchief.

NOTES

To confess and be hanged for his labor.

First to be hanged and then to confess—I tremble

at it. Nature would not invest herself in such shadowing   50

passion without some instruction. It is not

words that shakes me thus. Pish! Noses, ears, and

lips—is 't possible? Confess—handkerchief—O,

devil!   *He falls in a trance.*

IAGO Work on,   55

My medicine, work! Thus credulous fools are

  caught,

And many worthy and chaste dames even thus,

All guiltless, meet reproach.—What ho! My lord!

My lord, I say. Othello!   60

Enter Cassio.

How now, Cassio?

CASSIO What's the matter?

IAGO

My lord is fall'n into an epilepsy.

This is his second fit. He had one yesterday.

NOTES

CASSIO

Rub him about the temples. 65

IAGO No, forbear.

The lethargy must have his quiet course.

If not, he foams at mouth, and by and by

Breaks out to savage madness. Look, he stirs.

Do you withdraw yourself a little while. 70

He will recover straight. When he is gone,

I would on great occasion speak with you.

Cassio exits.

How is it, general? Have you not hurt your head?

OTHELLO

Dost thou mock me?

IAGO I mock you not, by heaven! 75

Would you would bear your fortune like a man!

OTHELLO

A hornèd man's a monster and a beast.

IAGO

There's many a beast, then, in a populous city,

And many a civil monster.

OTHELLO

Did he confess it? 80

NOTES

IAGO Good sir, be a man!

  Think every bearded fellow that's but yoked

  May draw with you. There's millions now alive

  That nightly lie in those unproper beds

  Which they dare swear peculiar. Your case is better.   85

  O, 'tis the spite of hell, the fiend's arch-mock,

  To lip a wanton in a secure couch

  And to suppose her chaste! No, let me know,

  And knowing what I am, I know what she shall be.

OTHELLO O, thou art wise, 'tis certain.   90

IAGO Stand you awhile apart.

  Confine yourself but in a patient list.

  Whilst you were here, o'erwhelmèd with your grief—

  A passion most unsuiting such a man—

  Cassio came hither. I shifted him away   95

  And laid good 'scuses upon your ecstasy,

  Bade him anon return and here speak with me,

  The which he promised. Do but encave yourself,

  And mark the fleers, the gibes, and notable scorns

  That dwell in every region of his face.   100

  For I will make him tell the tale anew—

  Where, how, how oft, how long ago, and when

NOTES

143

He hath and is again to cope your wife.

I say but mark his gesture. Marry, patience,

Or I shall say you're all in all in spleen,   105

And nothing of a man.

OTHELLO Dost thou hear, Iago,

I will be found most cunning in my patience,

But (dost thou hear?) most bloody.

IAGO That's not amiss.   110

But yet keep time in all. Will you withdraw?

Othello withdraws.

Now will I question Cassio of Bianca,

A huswife that by selling her desires

Buys herself bread and clothes. It is a creature

That dotes on Cassio—as 'tis the strumpet's plague   115

To beguile many and be beguiled by one.

He, when he hears of her, cannot restrain

From the excess of laughter. Here he comes.

Enter Cassio.

As he shall smile, Othello shall go mad,

And his unbookish jealousy must construe   120

NOTES

Poor Cassio's smiles, gestures, and light behaviors

Quite in the wrong.—How do you, lieutenant?

CASSIO

The worser that you give me the addition

Whose want even kills me.

IAGO

Ply Desdemona well, and you are sure on 't.   125

Now, if this suit lay in Bianca's power,

How quickly should you speed!

CASSIO, *laughing* Alas, poor caitiff!

OTHELLO Look how he laughs already!

IAGO I never knew woman love man so.   130

CASSIO

Alas, poor rogue, I think i' faith she loves me.

OTHELLO

Now he denies it faintly and laughs it out.

IAGO

Do you hear, Cassio?

OTHELLO Now he importunes him

To tell it o'er. Go to, well said, well said.   135

IAGO

She gives it out that you shall marry her.

NOTES

Do you intend it?

CASSIO Ha, ha, ha!

OTHELLO

Do you triumph, Roman? Do you triumph?

CASSIO I marry her? What, a customer? Prithee bear   140

some charity to my wit! Do not think it so unwholesome.

Ha, ha, ha!

OTHELLO So, so, so, so. They laugh that wins.

IAGO

Faith, the cry goes that you marry her.

CASSIO Prithee say true!   145

IAGO I am a very villain else.

OTHELLO Have you scored me? Well.

CASSIO This is the monkey's own giving out. She is

persuaded I will marry her out of her own love and

flattery, not out of my promise.   150

OTHELLO

Iago beckons me. Now he begins the story.

CASSIO She was here even now. She haunts me in

every place. I was the other day talking on the

sea-bank with certain Venetians, and thither comes

the bauble. By this hand, she falls thus about my   155

NOTES

neck!

OTHELLO Crying, "O dear Cassio," as it were; his

gesture imports it.

CASSIO So hangs and lolls and weeps upon me, so

shakes and pulls me. Ha, ha, ha!   160

OTHELLO Now he tells how she plucked him to my

chamber.—O, I see that nose of yours, but not that

dog I shall throw it to.

CASSIO Well, I must leave her company.

IAGO Before me, look where she comes.   165

Enter Bianca.

CASSIO 'Tis such another fitchew—marry, a perfumed

one!—What do you mean by this haunting

of me?

BIANCA Let the devil and his dam haunt you! What did

you mean by that same handkerchief you gave me   170

even now? I was a fine fool to take it! I must take

out the work? A likely piece of work, that you

should find it in your chamber and know not who

left it there! This is some minx's token, and I must

NOTES

take out the work! There, give it your hobbyhorse.   175

    Wheresoever you had it, I'll take out no work on 't.

CASSIO

    How now, my sweet Bianca? How now? How now?

OTHELLO

    By heaven, that should be my handkerchief!

BIANCA If you'll come to supper tonight you may. If

    you will not, come when you are next prepared   180

    for. *She exits.*

IAGO After her, after her!

CASSIO Faith, I must. She'll rail in the streets else.

IAGO Will you sup there?

CASSIO Faith, I intend so.   185

IAGO Well, I may chance to see you, for I would very

    fain speak with you.

CASSIO Prithee come. Will you?

IAGO Go to; say no more.   *Cassio exits.*

OTHELLO, *coming forward* How shall I murder him,   190

    Iago?

IAGO Did you perceive how he laughed at his vice?

OTHELLO O Iago!

IAGO And did you see the handkerchief?

NOTES

OTHELLO Was that mine?   195

IAGO Yours, by this hand! And to see how he prizes

the foolish woman your wife! She gave it him, and

he hath giv'n it his whore.

OTHELLO I would have him nine years a-killing! A fine

woman, a fair woman, a sweet woman!   200

IAGO Nay, you must forget that.

OTHELLO Ay, let her rot and perish and be damned

tonight, for she shall not live. No, my heart is turned

to stone. I strike it, and it hurts my hand. O, the

world hath not a sweeter creature! She might lie by   205

an emperor's side and command him tasks.

IAGO Nay, that's not your way.

OTHELLO Hang her, I do but say what she is! So

delicate with her needle, an admirable musician—

O, she will sing the savageness out of a bear!   210

Of so high and plenteous wit and invention!

IAGO She's the worse for all this.

OTHELLO O, a thousand, a thousand times!—And then

of so gentle a condition!

IAGO Ay, too gentle.   215

OTHELLO Nay, that's certain. But yet the pity of it,

NOTES

Iago! O, Iago, the pity of it, Iago!

IAGO If you are so fond over her iniquity, give her

    patent to offend, for if it touch not you, it comes

    near nobody.   220

OTHELLO I will chop her into messes! Cuckold me?

IAGO O, 'tis foul in her.

OTHELLO With mine officer!

IAGO That's fouler.

OTHELLO Get me some poison, Iago, this night. I'll not   225

    expostulate with her lest her body and beauty

    unprovide my mind again. This night, Iago.

IAGO Do it not with poison. Strangle her in her bed,

    even the bed she hath contaminated.

OTHELLO Good, good. The justice of it pleases. Very   230

    good.

IAGO And for Cassio, let me be his undertaker. You

    shall hear more by midnight.

OTHELLO

  Excellent good.   *A trumpet sounds.*

  What trumpet is that same?   235

IAGO I warrant something from Venice.

NOTES

'Tis Lodovico. This comes from the Duke.

See, your wife's with him.

LODOVICO God save you, worthy general.

OTHELLO With all my heart, sir.   240

LODOVICO

The Duke and the Senators of Venice greet you.

He hands Othello a paper.

OTHELLO

I kiss the instrument of their pleasures.

DESDEMONA

And what's the news, good cousin Lodovico?

IAGO

I am very glad to see you, signior.

Welcome to Cyprus.   245

LODOVICO

I thank you. How does Lieutenant Cassio?

IAGO Lives, sir.

DESDEMONA

Cousin, there's fall'n between him and my lord

An unkind breach, but you shall make all well.

NOTES

151

OTHELLO Are you sure of that?   250

DESDEMONA My lord?

OTHELLO, *reading* "This fail you not to do, as you

    will"—

LODOVICO

    He did not call; he's busy in the paper.

    Is there division 'twixt my lord and Cassio?   255

DESDEMONA

    A most unhappy one. I would do much

    T' atone them, for the love I bear to Cassio.

OTHELLO Fire and brimstone!

DESDEMONA My lord?

OTHELLO Are you wise?   260

DESDEMONA

    What, is he angry?

LODOVICO May be the letter moved him.

    For, as I think, they do command him home,

    Deputing Cassio in his government.

DESDEMONA By my troth, I am glad on 't.   265

OTHELLO Indeed?

DESDEMONA My lord?

OTHELLO I am glad to see you mad.

NOTES

DESDEMONA Why, sweet Othello!

OTHELLO, *striking her* Devil!   270

DESDEMONA I have not deserved this.

LODOVICO

  My lord, this would not be believed in Venice,

  Though I should swear I saw 't. 'Tis very much.

  Make her amends. She weeps.

OTHELLO O, devil, devil!   275

  If that the Earth could teem with woman's tears,

  Each drop she falls would prove a crocodile.

  Out of my sight!

DESDEMONA I will not stay to offend you.

                                                                  She begins to leave.

LODOVICO Truly an obedient lady.   280

  I do beseech your Lordship call her back.

OTHELLO Mistress.

DESDEMONA, *turning back* My lord?

OTHELLO What would you with her, sir?

LODOVICO Who, I, my lord?   285

OTHELLO

  Ay, you did wish that I would make her turn.

  Sir, she can turn, and turn, and yet go on,

NOTES

And turn again. And she can weep, sir, weep.

And she's obedient, as you say, obedient.

Very obedient.—Proceed you in your tears.—   290

Concerning this, sir—O, well-painted passion!—

I am commanded home.—Get you away.

I'll send for you anon.—Sir, I obey the mandate

And will return to Venice.—Hence, avaunt!

Desdemona exits.

Cassio shall have my place. And, sir, tonight   295

I do entreat that we may sup together.

You are welcome, sir, to Cyprus. Goats and

  monkeys!   *He exits.*

LODOVICO

Is this the noble Moor, whom our full senate

Call all in all sufficient? Is this the nature   300

Whom passion could not shake, whose solid virtue

The shot of accident nor dart of chance

Could neither graze nor pierce?

IAGO He is much

  changed.   305

LODOVICO

Are his wits safe? Is he not light of brain?

NOTES

IAGO

He's that he is. I may not breathe my censure

What he might be. If what he might he is not,

I would to heaven he were.

LODOVICO What? Strike his wife?   310

IAGO

'Faith, that was not so well. Yet would I knew

That stroke would prove the worst.

LODOVICO Is it his use?

Or did the letters work upon his blood

And new-create this fault?   315

IAGO Alas, alas!

It is not honesty in me to speak

What I have seen and known. You shall observe

    him,

And his own courses will denote him so   320

That I may save my speech. Do but go after

And mark how he continues.

LODOVICO

I am sorry that I am deceived in him.

They exit.

NOTES

<u>**NOTES**</u>

Scene 2

Enter Othello and Emilia.

OTHELLO You have seen nothing then?

EMILIA

  Nor ever heard, nor ever did suspect.

OTHELLO

  Yes, you have seen Cassio and she together.

EMILIA

  But then I saw no harm, and then I heard

  Each syllable that breath made up between them.   5

OTHELLO

  What, did they never whisper?

EMILIA Never, my lord.

OTHELLO Nor send you out o' th' way?

EMILIA Never.

OTHELLO

  To fetch her fan, her gloves, her mask, nor nothing?   10

EMILIA Never, my lord.

OTHELLO That's strange.

EMILIA

  I durst, my lord, to wager she is honest,

NOTES

Lay down my soul at stake. If you think other,

Remove your thought. It doth abuse your bosom.   15

If any wretch have put this in your head,

Let heaven requite it with the serpent's curse,

For if she be not honest, chaste, and true,

There's no man happy. The purest of their wives

Is foul as slander.   20

OTHELLO Bid her come hither. Go.

Emilia exits.

She says enough. Yet she's a simple bawd

That cannot say as much. This is a subtle whore,

A closet lock and key of villainous secrets.

And yet she'll kneel and pray. I have seen her do 't.   25

Enter Desdemona and Emilia.

DESDEMONA My lord, what is your will?

OTHELLO

Pray you, chuck, come hither.

DESDEMONA What is your

pleasure?

NOTES

OTHELLO

Let me see your eyes. Look in my face.   30

DESDEMONA What horrible fancy's this?

OTHELLO, *to Emilia* Some of your function,

mistress.

Leave procreants alone, and shut the door.

Cough, or cry "hem," if anybody come.   35

Your mystery, your mystery! Nay, dispatch.

Emilia exits.

DESDEMONA, *kneeling*

Upon my knees, what doth your speech import?

I understand a fury in your words,

But not the words.

OTHELLO Why? What art thou?   40

DESDEMONA

Your wife, my lord, your true and loyal wife.

OTHELLO Come, swear it. Damn thyself,

Lest, being like one of heaven, the devils themselves

Should fear to seize thee. Therefore be double

damned.   45

Swear thou art honest.

DESDEMONA Heaven doth truly know it.

NOTES

OTHELLO

Heaven truly knows that thou art false as hell.

DESDEMONA, *standing*

To whom, my lord? With whom? How am I false?

OTHELLO

Ah, Desdemon, away, away, away!　　　　　　　　　50

DESDEMONA

Alas the heavy day, why do you weep?

Am I the motive of these tears, my lord?

If haply you my father do suspect

An instrument of this your calling back,

Lay not your blame on me. If you have lost him,　　55

I have lost him too.

OTHELLO Had it pleased heaven

To try me with affliction, had they rained

All kind of sores and shames on my bare head,

Steeped me in poverty to the very lips,　　　　　　60

Given to captivity me and my utmost hopes,

I should have found in some place of my soul

A drop of patience. But alas, to make me

A fixèd figure for the time of scorn

To point his slow unmoving finger at—　　　　　　65

NOTES

Yet could I bear that too, well, very well.

But there where I have garnered up my heart,

Where either I must live or bear no life,

The fountain from the which my current runs

Or else dries up—to be discarded thence,   70

Or keep it as a cistern for foul toads

To knot and gender in—turn thy complexion there,

Patience, thou young and rose-lipped cherubin,

Ay, there look grim as hell.

DESDEMONA

I hope my noble lord esteems me honest.   75

OTHELLO

O, ay, as summer flies are in the shambles,

That quicken even with blowing! O thou weed,

Who art so lovely fair, and smell'st so sweet

That the sense aches at thee, would thou hadst

ne'er been born!   80

DESDEMONA

Alas, what ignorant sin have I committed?

OTHELLO

Was this fair paper, this most goodly book,

Made to write "whore" upon? What committed?

NOTES

Committed? O thou public commoner,

I should make very forges of my cheeks   85

That would to cinders burn up modesty,

Did I but speak thy deeds. What committed?

Heaven stops the nose at it, and the moon winks;

The bawdy wind that kisses all it meets

Is hushed within the hollow mine of earth   90

And will not hear 't. What committed?

Impudent strumpet!

DESDEMONA By heaven, you do me wrong!

OTHELLO Are not you a strumpet?

DESDEMONA No, as I am a Christian!   95

If to preserve this vessel for my lord

From any other foul unlawful touch

Be not to be a strumpet, I am none.

OTHELLO What, not a whore?

DESDEMONA No, as I shall be saved.   100

OTHELLO Is 't possible?

DESDEMONA

O, heaven forgive us!

OTHELLO I cry you mercy, then.

I took you for that cunning whore of Venice

NOTES

That married with Othello.—You, mistress,   105

Enter Emilia.

That have the office opposite to Saint Peter

And keeps the gate of hell—you, you, ay, you!

We have done our course. There's money for your

   pains.   *He gives her money.*

I pray you turn the key and keep our counsel.   110

                                                 He exits.

EMILIA

   Alas, what does this gentleman conceive?

   How do you, madam? How do you, my good lady?

DESDEMONA Faith, half asleep.

EMILIA

   Good madam, what's the matter with my lord?

DESDEMONA With who?   115

EMILIA Why, with my lord, madam.

DESDEMONA

   Who is thy lord?

EMILIA He that is yours, sweet lady.

NOTES

DESDEMONA

I have none. Do not talk to me, Emilia.

I cannot weep, nor answers have I none   120

But what should go by water. Prithee, tonight

Lay on my bed my wedding sheets. Remember.

And call thy husband hither.

EMILIA Here's a change indeed.   *She exits.*

DESDEMONA

'Tis meet I should be used so, very meet.   125

How have I been behaved that he might stick

The small'st opinion on my least misuse?

Enter Iago and Emilia.

IAGO

What is your pleasure, madam? How is 't with you?

DESDEMONA

I cannot tell. Those that do teach young babes

Do it with gentle means and easy tasks.   130

He might have chid me so, for, in good faith,

I am a child to chiding.

IAGO What is the matter, lady?

NOTES

EMILIA

Alas, Iago, my lord hath so bewhored her,

Thrown such despite and heavy terms upon her   135

As true hearts cannot bear.

DESDEMONA

Am I that name, Iago?

IAGO What name, fair

lady?

DESDEMONA

Such as she said my lord did say I was.   140

EMILIA

He called her "whore." A beggar in his drink

Could not have laid such terms upon his callet.

IAGO Why did he so?

DESDEMONA

I do not know. I am sure I am none such.

IAGO

Do not weep, do not weep! Alas the day!   145

EMILIA

Hath she forsook so many noble matches,

Her father and her country and her friends,

To be called "whore"? Would it not make one

NOTES

weep?

DESDEMONA It is my wretched fortune.   150

IAGO

Beshrew him for 't! How comes this trick upon him?

DESDEMONA Nay, heaven doth know.

EMILIA

I will be hanged if some eternal villain,

Some busy and insinuating rogue,

Some cogging, cozening slave, to get some office,   155

Have not devised this slander. I will be hanged else.

IAGO

Fie, there is no such man. It is impossible.

DESDEMONA

If any such there be, heaven pardon him.

EMILIA

A halter pardon him, and hell gnaw his bones!

Why should he call her "whore"? Who keeps her   160

    company?

What place? What time? What form? What

    likelihood?

The Moor's abused by some most villainous knave,

Some base notorious knave, some scurvy fellow.   165

NOTES

O heaven, that such companions thou 'dst unfold,

And put in every honest hand a whip

To lash the rascals naked through the world,

Even from the east to th' west!

IAGO Speak within door.   170

EMILIA

O, fie upon them! Some such squire he was

That turned your wit the seamy side without

And made you to suspect me with the Moor.

IAGO

You are a fool. Go to!

DESDEMONA Alas, Iago,   175

What shall I do to win my lord again?

Good friend, go to him. For by this light of heaven,

I know not how I lost him. *She kneels.* Here I

   kneel.

If e'er my will did trespass 'gainst his love,   180

Either in discourse of thought or actual deed,

Or that mine eyes, mine ears, or any sense

Delighted them in any other form,

Or that I do not yet, and ever did,

And ever will—though he do shake me off   185

NOTES

To beggarly divorcement—love him dearly,

Comfort forswear me! *She stands.* Unkindness may

   do much,

And his unkindness may defeat my life,

But never taint my love. I cannot say "whore"—   190

It does abhor me now I speak the word.

To do the act that might the addition earn,

Not the world's mass of vanity could make me.

IAGO

I pray you be content. 'Tis but his humor.

The business of the state does him offense,   195

And he does chide with you.

DESDEMONA

If 'twere no other—

IAGO It is but so, I warrant.

Trumpets sound.

Hark how these instruments summon to supper.

The messengers of Venice stays the meat.   200

Go in and weep not. All things shall be well.

Desdemona and Emilia exit.

Enter Roderigo.

NOTES

How now, Roderigo?

RODERIGO I do not find

That thou deal'st justly with me.

IAGO What in the contrary?   205

RODERIGO Every day thou daff'st me with some device,

Iago, and rather, as it seems to me now,

keep'st from me all conveniency than suppliest me

with the least advantage of hope. I will indeed no

longer endure it. Nor am I yet persuaded to put up   210

in peace what already I have foolishly suffered.

IAGO Will you hear me, Roderigo?

RODERIGO Faith, I have heard too much, and your

words and performances are no kin together.

IAGO You charge me most unjustly.   215

RODERIGO With naught but truth. I have wasted myself

out of my means. The jewels you have had

from me to deliver to Desdemona would half have

corrupted a votaress. You have told me she hath

received them, and returned me expectations and   220

comforts of sudden respect and acquaintance, but I

find none.

NOTES

IAGO Well, go to! Very well.

RODERIGO "Very well." "Go to!" I cannot go to, man,

nor 'tis not very well! By this hand, I say 'tis very   225

scurvy, and begin to find myself fopped in it.

IAGO Very well.

RODERIGO I tell you 'tis not very well! I will make

myself known to Desdemona. If she will return me

my jewels, I will give over my suit and repent my   230

unlawful solicitation. If not, assure yourself I will

seek satisfaction of you.

IAGO You have said now.

RODERIGO Ay, and said nothing but what I protest

intendment of doing.   235

IAGO Why, now I see there's mettle in thee, and even

from this instant do build on thee a better opinion

than ever before. Give me thy hand, Roderigo.

Thou hast taken against me a most just exception,

but yet I protest I have dealt most directly in thy   240

affair.

RODERIGO It hath not appeared.

IAGO I grant indeed it hath not appeared, and your

suspicion is not without wit and judgment. But,

NOTES

170

Roderigo, if thou hast that in thee indeed which I   245

have greater reason to believe now than ever—I

mean purpose, courage, and valor—this night show

it. If thou the next night following enjoy not Desdemona,

take me from this world with treachery and

devise engines for my life.   250

RODERIGO Well, what is it? Is it within reason and

compass?

IAGO Sir, there is especial commission come from

Venice to depute Cassio in Othello's place.

RODERIGO Is that true? Why, then, Othello and Desdemona   255

return again to Venice.

IAGO O, no. He goes into Mauritania and takes away

with him the fair Desdemona, unless his abode be

lingered here by some accident—wherein none

can be so determinate as the removing of Cassio.   260

RODERIGO How do you mean, removing him?

IAGO Why, by making him uncapable of Othello's

place: knocking out his brains.

RODERIGO And that you would have me to do?

IAGO Ay, if you dare do yourself a profit and a right. He   265

sups tonight with a harlotry, and thither will I go to

NOTES

him. He knows not yet of his honorable fortune. If you will watch his going thence (which I will fashion to fall out between twelve and one), you may take him at your pleasure. I will be near to second 270
your attempt, and he shall fall between us. Come, stand not amazed at it, but go along with me. I will show you such a necessity in his death that you shall think yourself bound to put it on him. It is now high supper time, and the night grows to waste. About it! 275

RODERIGO I will hear further reason for this.

IAGO And you shall be satisfied.

They exit.

NOTES

Scene 3

Enter Othello, Lodovico, Desdemona, Emilia, and

Attendants.

LODOVICO

I do beseech you, sir, trouble yourself no further.

OTHELLO

O, pardon me, 'twill do me good to walk.

LODOVICO

Madam, good night. I humbly thank your Ladyship.

DESDEMONA Your Honor is most welcome.

OTHELLO

Will you walk, sir?—O, Desdemona—   5

DESDEMONA My lord?

OTHELLO Get you to bed on th' instant. I will be

   returned forthwith. Dismiss your attendant there.

   Look 't be done.

DESDEMONA I will, my lord.   10

All but Desdemona and Emilia exit.

EMILIA

How goes it now? He looks gentler than he did.

NOTES

DESDEMONA

He says he will return incontinent,

And hath commanded me to go to bed,

And bade me to dismiss you.

EMILIA Dismiss me?   15

DESDEMONA

It was his bidding. Therefore, good Emilia,

Give me my nightly wearing, and adieu.

We must not now displease him.

EMILIA I would you had never seen him.

DESDEMONA

So would not I. My love doth so approve him   20

That even his stubbornness, his checks, his frowns—

Prithee, unpin me—have grace and favor in them.

EMILIA

I have laid those sheets you bade me on the bed.

DESDEMONA

All's one. Good faith, how foolish are our minds!

If I do die before thee, prithee, shroud me   25

In one of those same sheets.

EMILIA Come, come, you talk!

DESDEMONA

NOTES

My mother had a maid called Barbary.

She was in love, and he she loved proved mad

And did forsake her. She had a song of willow,   30

An old thing 'twas, but it expressed her fortune,

And she died singing it. That song tonight

Will not go from my mind. I have much to do

But to go hang my head all at one side

And sing it like poor Barbary. Prithee, dispatch.   35

EMILIA Shall I go fetch your nightgown?

DESDEMONA No, unpin me here.

   This Lodovico is a proper man.

EMILIA A very handsome man.

DESDEMONA He speaks well.   40

EMILIA I know a lady in Venice would have walked

   barefoot to Palestine for a touch of his nether lip.

DESDEMONA, *singing*

> *The poor soul sat sighing by a sycamore tree,*
>
> > *Sing all a green willow.*
>
> *Her hand on her bosom, her head on her knee,*   45
>
> > *Sing willow, willow, willow.*
>
> *The fresh streams ran by her and murmured her*

moans,

NOTES

Sing willow, willow, willow;

Her salt tears fell from her, and softened the　　　　50

stones—

Lay by these.

Sing willow, willow, willow.

Prithee hie thee! He'll come anon.

Sing all a green willow must be my garland.　　　　55

Let nobody blame him, his scorn I approve.

Nay, that's not next. Hark, who is 't that knocks?

EMILIA It's the wind.

DESDEMONA

I called my love false love, but what said he then?

Sing willow, willow, willow.　　　　60

If I court more women, you'll couch with more

men.—

So, get thee gone. Good night. Mine eyes do itch;

Doth that bode weeping?

EMILIA 'Tis neither here nor there.　　　　65

DESDEMONA

I have heard it said so. O these men, these men!

Dost thou in conscience think—tell me, Emilia—

That there be women do abuse their husbands

NOTES

In such gross kind?

EMILIA There be some such, no   70

question.

DESDEMONA

Wouldst thou do such a deed for all the world?

EMILIA

Why, would not you?

DESDEMONA No, by this heavenly light!

EMILIA

Nor I neither, by this heavenly light.   75

I might do 't as well i' th' dark.

DESDEMONA

Wouldst thou do such a deed for all the world?

EMILIA The world's a huge thing. It is a great price

for a small vice.

DESDEMONA In troth, I think thou wouldst not.   80

EMILIA In troth, I think I should, and undo 't when I

had done it. Marry, I would not do such a thing for

a joint ring, nor for measures of lawn, nor for

gowns, petticoats, nor caps, nor any petty exhibition.

But for the whole world—'Uds pity! Who   85

would not make her husband a cuckold to make

NOTES

him a monarch? I should venture purgatory for 't.

DESDEMONA Beshrew me if I would do such a wrong

   for the whole world!

EMILIA Why, the wrong is but a wrong i' th' world;   90

   and, having the world for your labor, 'tis a wrong in

   your own world, and you might quickly make it

   right.

DESDEMONA I do not think there is any such woman.

EMILIA Yes, a dozen; and as many to th' vantage as   95

   would store the world they played for.

 But I do think it is their husbands' faults

 If wives do fall. Say that they slack their duties,

 And pour our treasures into foreign laps;

 Or else break out in peevish jealousies,   100

 Throwing restraint upon us. Or say they strike us,

 Or scant our former having in despite.

 Why, we have galls, and though we have some grace,

 Yet have we some revenge. Let husbands know

 Their wives have sense like them. They see, and   105

    smell,

 And have their palates both for sweet and sour,

 As husbands have. What is it that they do

NOTES

When they change us for others? Is it sport?

I think it is. And doth affection breed it?   110

I think it doth. Is 't frailty that thus errs?

It is so too. And have not we affections,

Desires for sport, and frailty, as men have?

Then let them use us well. Else let them know,

The ills we do, their ills instruct us so.   115

DESDEMONA

Good night, good night. God me such uses send,

Not to pick bad from bad, but by bad mend.

They exit.

NOTES

ACT 5

Scene 1

Enter Iago and Roderigo.

IAGO

Here, stand behind this bulk. Straight will he

  come.

Wear thy good rapier bare, and put it home.

Quick, quick! Fear nothing. I'll be at thy elbow.

It makes us or it mars us—think on that,   5

And fix most firm thy resolution.

RODERIGO

Be near at hand. I may miscarry in 't.

IAGO

Here, at thy hand. Be bold and take thy stand.

He moves aside.

RODERIGO

I have no great devotion to the deed,

And yet he hath given me satisfying reasons.   10

'Tis but a man gone. Forth, my sword! He dies.

NOTES

IAGO, *aside*

 I have rubbed this young quat almost to the sense,

 And he grows angry. Now, whether he kill Cassio,

 Or Cassio him, or each do kill the other,

 Every way makes my gain. Live Roderigo,   15

 He calls me to a restitution large

 Of gold and jewels that I bobbed from him

 As gifts to Desdemona.

 It must not be. If Cassio do remain,

 He hath a daily beauty in his life   20

 That makes me ugly. And besides, the Moor

 May unfold me to him. There stand I in much peril.

 No, he must die. Be 't so. I hear him coming.

Enter Cassio.

RODERIGO

 I know his gait. 'Tis he!—Villain, thou diest!

He thrusts at Cassio.

CASSIO

 That thrust had been mine enemy indeed   25

NOTES

But that my coat is better than thou know'st.

I will make proof of thine.

He draws, and stabs Roderigo.

RODERIGO O, I am slain!

Roderigo falls.

Iago stabs Cassio in the leg, and exits.

CASSIO

I am maimed forever! Help, ho! Murder, murder!

Enter Othello.

OTHELLO

The voice of Cassio! Iago keeps his word.   30

RODERIGO O, villain that I am!

OTHELLO, *aside* It is even so.

CASSIO O, help ho! Light! A surgeon!

OTHELLO, *aside*

'Tis he! O brave Iago, honest and just,

That hast such noble sense of thy friend's wrong!   35

Thou teachest me.—Minion, your dear lies dead,

And your unblest fate hies. Strumpet, I come.

Forth of my heart those charms, thine eyes, are

NOTES

blotted.

Thy bed, lust-stained, shall with lust's blood be   40

    spotted.   *Othello exits.*

Enter Lodovico and Gratiano.

CASSIO

    What ho! No watch? No passage? Murder, murder!

GRATIANO

    'Tis some mischance. The voice is very direful.

CASSIO O, help!

LODOVICO Hark!   45

RODERIGO O wretched villain!

LODOVICO

    Two or three groan. 'Tis heavy night.

    These may be counterfeits. Let's think 't unsafe

    To come in to the cry without more help.

RODERIGO

    Nobody come? Then shall I bleed to death.   50

Enter Iago with a light.

NOTES

LODOVICO Hark!

GRATIANO

Here's one comes in his shirt, with light and

weapons.

IAGO

Who's there? Whose noise is this that cries on

murder?   55

LODOVICO

We do not know.

IAGO Did not you hear a cry?

CASSIO

Here, here! For heaven's sake, help me!

IAGO What's the matter?

GRATIANO, *to Lodovico*

This is Othello's ancient, as I take it.   60

LODOVICO

The same indeed, a very valiant fellow.

IAGO, *to Cassio*

What are you here that cry so grievously?

CASSIO

Iago? O, I am spoiled, undone by villains.

Give me some help!

NOTES

IAGO

O me, lieutenant! What villains have done this?   65

CASSIO

I think that one of them is hereabout

And cannot make away.

IAGO O treacherous villains!

To Lodovico and Gratiano. What are you there?

Come in, and give some help.   70

RODERIGO O, help me here!

CASSIO

That's one of them.

IAGO*, to Roderigo* O murd'rous slave! O villain!

He stabs Roderigo.

RODERIGO

O damned Iago! O inhuman dog!

IAGO

Kill men i' th' dark?—Where be these bloody   75

   thieves?

How silent is this town! Ho, murder, murder!—

What may you be? Are you of good or evil?

LODOVICO

As you shall prove us, praise us.

NOTES

IAGO Signior Lodovico?   80

LODOVICO He, sir.

IAGO

I cry you mercy. Here's Cassio hurt by villains.

GRATIANO Cassio?

IAGO

How is 't, brother?

CASSIO My leg is cut in two.   85

IAGO Marry, heaven forbid!

Light, gentlemen. I'll bind it with my shirt.

Enter Bianca.

BIANCA

What is the matter, ho? Who is 't that cried?

IAGO

Who is 't that cried?

BIANCA O, my dear Cassio,   90

My sweet Cassio! O Cassio, Cassio, Cassio!

IAGO

O notable strumpet! Cassio, may you suspect

Who they should be that have thus mangled you?

NOTES

CASSIO No.

GRATIANO

I am sorry to find you thus; I have been to seek you.   95

IAGO

Lend me a garter. So.—O for a chair

To bear him easily hence!

BIANCA

Alas, he faints. O, Cassio, Cassio, Cassio!

IAGO

Gentlemen all, I do suspect this trash

To be a party in this injury.—   100

Patience awhile, good Cassio.—Come, come;

Lend me a light. *Peering at Roderigo.* Know we this

   face or no?

Alas, my friend and my dear countryman

Roderigo? No! Yes, sure. O heaven, Roderigo!   105

GRATIANO What, of Venice?

IAGO Even he, sir. Did you know him?

GRATIANO Know him? Ay.

IAGO

Signior Gratiano? I cry your gentle pardon.

These bloody accidents must excuse my manners   110

NOTES

That so neglected you.

GRATIANO I am glad to see you.

IAGO

How do you, Cassio?—O, a chair, a chair!

GRATIANO Roderigo?

IAGO

He, he, 'tis he! *A chair is brought in.* O, that's well   115

  said; the chair.—

Some good man bear him carefully from hence.

I'll fetch the General's surgeon.— For you, mistress,

Save you your labor.—He that lies slain here,

  Cassio,   120

Was my dear friend. What malice was between you?

CASSIO

None in the world. Nor do I know the man.

IAGO, *to Bianca*

What, look you pale?—O, bear him out o' th' air.

                           Cassio, in the chair, and Roderigo are carried off.

To Gratiano and Lodovico. Stay you, good

  gentlemen.—Look you pale, mistress?—   125

Do you perceive the gastness of her eye?—

Nay, if you stare, we shall hear more anon.—

NOTES

Behold her well. I pray you, look upon her.

Do you see, gentlemen? Nay, guiltiness will speak

Though tongues were out of use.   130

Enter Emilia.

EMILIA

Alas, what is the matter? What is the matter,

husband?

IAGO

Cassio hath here been set on in the dark

By Roderigo and fellows that are scaped.

He's almost slain, and Roderigo dead.   135

EMILIA

Alas, good gentleman! Alas, good Cassio!

IAGO

This is the fruits of whoring. Prithee, Emilia,

Go know of Cassio where he supped tonight.

To Bianca. What, do you shake at that?

BIANCA

He supped at my house, but I therefore shake not. 140

IAGO

NOTES

O, did he so? I charge you go with me.

EMILIA O fie upon thee, strumpet!

BIANCA

I am no strumpet, but of life as honest

As you that thus abuse me.

EMILIA As I? Faugh! Fie upon thee!   145

IAGO

Kind gentlemen, let's go see poor Cassio dressed.—

Come, mistress, you must tell 's another tale.—

Emilia, run you to the citadel

And tell my lord and lady what hath happed.—

Will you go on afore? *Aside.* This is the night   150

That either makes me or fordoes me quite.

They exit in different directions.

NOTES

Enter Othello with a light, and Desdemona in her bed.

OTHELLO

It is the cause, it is the cause, my soul.

Let me not name it to you, you chaste stars.

It is the cause. Yet I'll not shed her blood,

Nor scar that whiter skin of hers than snow,

And smooth as monumental alabaster.   5

Yet she must die, else she'll betray more men.

Put out the light, and then put out the light.

If I quench thee, thou flaming minister,

I can again thy former light restore

Should I repent me. But once put out thy light,   10

Thou cunning'st pattern of excelling nature,

I know not where is that Promethean heat

That can thy light relume. When I have plucked the

   rose,

I cannot give it vital growth again.   15

It needs must wither. I'll smell it on the tree.

O balmy breath, that dost almost persuade

Justice to break her sword! *He kisses her.* One

NOTES

more, one more.

Be thus when thou art dead, and I will kill thee   20

And love thee after. One more, and this the last.

He kisses her.

So sweet was ne'er so fatal. I must weep,

But they are cruel tears. This sorrow's heavenly:

It strikes where it doth love. She wakes.

DESDEMONA

Who's there? Othello?   25

OTHELLO Ay, Desdemona.

DESDEMONA Will you come to bed, my lord?

OTHELLO

Have you prayed tonight, Desdemon?

DESDEMONA Ay, my lord.

OTHELLO

If you bethink yourself of any crime   30

Unreconciled as yet to heaven and grace,

Solicit for it straight.

DESDEMONA Alack, my lord,

What may you mean by that?

OTHELLO

Well, do it, and be brief. I will walk by.   35

NOTES

I would not kill thy unprepmeasurèd spirit.

No, heaven forfend! I would not kill thy soul.

DESDEMONA Talk you of killing?

OTHELLO

Ay, I do.

DESDEMONA Then heaven have mercy on me.   40

OTHELLO Amen, with all my heart.

DESDEMONA

If you say so, I hope you will not kill me.

OTHELLO Humh.

DESDEMONA

And yet I fear you, for you're fatal then

When your eyes roll so. Why I should fear I know   45

   not,

Since guiltiness I know not, but yet I feel I fear.

OTHELLO

Think on thy sins.

DESDEMONA They are loves I bear to you.

OTHELLO Ay, and for that thou diest.   50

DESDEMONA

That death's unnatural that kills for loving.

Alas, why gnaw you so your nether lip?

NOTES

Some bloody passion shakes your very frame.

These are portents, but yet I hope, I hope

They do not point on me.   55

OTHELLO Peace, and be still.

DESDEMONA

I will so. What's the matter?

OTHELLO That handkerchief

Which I so loved, and gave thee, thou gav'st to

Cassio.   60

DESDEMONA

No, by my life and soul! Send for the man

And ask him.

OTHELLO

Sweet soul, take heed, take heed of perjury.

Thou art on thy deathbed.

DESDEMONA

Ay, but not yet to die.   65

OTHELLO Yes, presently.

Therefore confess thee freely of thy sin.

For to deny each article with oath

Cannot remove nor choke the strong conception

That I do groan withal. Thou art to die.   70

NOTES

DESDEMONA

Then Lord have mercy on me!

OTHELLO I say "Amen."

DESDEMONA

And have you mercy, too. I never did

Offend you in my life, never loved Cassio

But with such general warranty of heaven   75

As I might love. I never gave him token.

OTHELLO

By heaven, I saw my handkerchief in 's hand!

O perjured woman, thou dost stone my heart

And mak'st me call what I intend to do

A murder, which I thought a sacrifice!   80

I saw the handkerchief!

DESDEMONA He found it, then.

I never gave it him. Send for him hither.

Let him confess a truth.

OTHELLO He hath confessed.   85

DESDEMONA What, my lord?

OTHELLO

That he hath used thee.

DESDEMONA How? Unlawfully?

NOTES

OTHELLO Ay.

DESDEMONA

He will not say so.   90

OTHELLO No. His mouth is stopped.

Honest Iago hath ta'en order for 't.

DESDEMONA

O, my fear interprets. What, is he dead?

OTHELLO

Had all his hairs been lives, my great revenge

Had stomach for them all.   95

DESDEMONA

Alas, he is betrayed, and I undone.   *She weeps.*

OTHELLO

Out, strumpet! Weep'st thou for him to my face?

DESDEMONA

O banish me, my lord, but kill me not!

OTHELLO Down, strumpet!

DESDEMONA

Kill me tomorrow, let me live tonight.   100

OTHELLO Nay, if you strive—

DESDEMONA

But half an hour!

NOTES

OTHELLO Being done, there is no pause.

DESDEMONA

   But while I say one prayer!

OTHELLO It is too late.   105

                                                        He smothers her.

EMILIA, *within*

   My lord, my lord? What ho! My lord, my lord!

OTHELLO

   What noise is this?—Not dead? Not yet quite dead?

   I that am cruel am yet merciful.

   I would not have thee linger in thy pain.

   So, so.   110

EMILIA, *within* What, ho! My lord, my lord!

OTHELLO Who's

   there?

EMILIA, *within*

   O, good my lord, I would speak a word with you.

OTHELLO

   Yes. 'Tis Emilia.—By and by.—She's dead.   115

   'Tis like she comes to speak of Cassio's death.

   The noise was here. Ha, no more moving?

   Still as the grave. Shall she come in? Were 't good?

NOTES

197

I think she stirs again. No. What's best to do?

If she come in, she'll sure speak to my wife.   120

My wife, my wife! What wife? I have no wife.

O insupportable! O heavy hour!

Methinks it should be now a huge eclipse

Of sun and moon, and that th' affrighted globe

Should yawn at alteration.   125

EMILIA, *within* I do beseech you

That I may speak with you. O, good my lord—

OTHELLO

I had forgot thee. O, come in, Emilia.—

Soft, by and by, let me the curtains draw.—

Where art thou?   130

Enter Emilia.

What's the matter with thee now?

EMILIA

O, my good lord, yonder's foul murders done.

OTHELLO What? Now?

EMILIA But now, my lord.

NOTES

OTHELLO

It is the very error of the moon. 135

She comes more nearer Earth than she was wont

And makes men mad.

EMILIA Cassio, my lord, hath killed

A young Venetian called Roderigo.

OTHELLO

Roderigo killed? And Cassio killed? 140

EMILIA No, Cassio is not killed.

OTHELLO

Not Cassio killed? Then murder's out of tune,

And sweet revenge grows harsh.

DESDEMONA O falsely, falsely murdered.

EMILIA

O Lord, what cry is that? 145

OTHELLO That? What?

EMILIA

Out, and alas, that was my lady's voice!

Help! Help ho! Help! O lady, speak again!

Sweet Desdemona, O sweet mistress, speak!

DESDEMONA A guiltless death I die. 150

EMILIA O, who hath done this deed?

NOTES

DESDEMONA Nobody. I myself. Farewell.

Commend me to my kind lord. O, farewell.

She dies.

OTHELLO

Why, how should she be murdered?

EMILIA Alas, who   155

knows?

OTHELLO

You heard her say herself, it was not I.

EMILIA

She said so. I must needs report the truth.

OTHELLO

She's like a liar gone to burning hell!

'Twas I that killed her.   160

EMILIA

O, the more angel she, and you the blacker devil!

OTHELLO

She turned to folly, and she was a whore.

EMILIA

Thou dost belie her, and thou art a devil!

OTHELLO She was false as water.

EMILIA Thou art rash as fire to say   165

NOTES

That she was false. O, she was heavenly true!

OTHELLO

Cassio did top her. Ask thy husband else.

O, I were damned beneath all depth in hell

But that I did proceed upon just grounds

To this extremity. Thy husband knew it all.   170

EMILIA My husband?

OTHELLO Thy husband.

EMILIA That she was false to wedlock?

OTHELLO

Ay, with Cassio. Had she been true,

If heaven would make me such another world   175

Of one entire and perfect chrysolite,

I'd not have sold her for it.

EMILIA My husband?

OTHELLO

Ay, 'twas he that told me on her first.

An honest man he is, and hates the slime   180

That sticks on filthy deeds.

EMILIA My husband?

OTHELLO

What needs this iterance, woman? I say, thy

NOTES

husband.

EMILIA

O mistress, villainy hath made mocks with love!— 185

My husband say she was false?

OTHELLO He, woman.

I say thy husband. Dost understand the word?

My friend, thy husband; honest, honest Iago.

EMILIA

If he say so, may his pernicious soul 190

Rot half a grain a day! He lies to th' heart!

She was too fond of her most filthy bargain.

He draws his sword.

OTHELLO Hah?

EMILIA Do thy worst!

This deed of thine is no more worthy heaven 195

Than thou wast worthy her.

OTHELLO Peace, you were best!

EMILIA

Thou hast not half that power to do me harm

As I have to be hurt. O gull! O dolt,

As ignorant as dirt! Thou hast done a deed— 200

I care not for thy sword. I'll make thee known,

NOTES

Though I lost twenty lives. Help! Help, ho! Help!

The Moor hath killed my mistress! Murder, murder!

Enter Montano, Gratiano, and Iago.

MONTANO

What is the matter? How now, general?

EMILIA

O, are you come, Iago? You have done well,   205

That men must lay their murders on your neck.

GRATIANO What is the matter?

EMILIA, *to Iago*

Disprove this villain, if thou be'st a man.

He says thou told'st him that his wife was false.

I know thou didst not. Thou 'rt not such a villain.   210

Speak, for my heart is full.

IAGO

I told him what I thought, and told no more

Than what he found himself was apt and true.

EMILIA

But did you ever tell him she was false?

IAGO I did.   215

NOTES

EMILIA

You told a lie, an odious, damnèd lie!

Upon my soul, a lie, a wicked lie!

She false with Cassio? Did you say with Cassio?

IAGO

With Cassio, mistress. Go to! Charm your tongue.

EMILIA

I will not charm my tongue. I am bound to speak.   220

My mistress here lies murdered in her bed.

ALL O heavens forfend!

EMILIA, *to Iago*

And your reports have set the murder on!

OTHELLO

Nay, stare not, masters; it is true indeed.

GRATIANO 'Tis a strange truth.   225

MONTANO

O monstrous act!

EMILIA Villainy, villainy, villainy!

I think upon 't, I think! I smell 't! O villainy!

I thought so then. I'll kill myself for grief!

O villainy! Villainy!   230

NOTES

IAGO

What, are you mad? I charge you get you home.

EMILIA

Good gentlemen, let me have leave to speak.

'Tis proper I obey him, but not now.

Perchance, Iago, I will ne'er go home.

OTHELLO

O, O, O!   *Othello falls on the bed.* 235

EMILIA Nay, lay thee down, and roar!

For thou hast killed the sweetest innocent

That e'er did lift up eye.

OTHELLO, *standing* O, she was foul!—

I scarce did know you, uncle. There lies your niece,   240

Whose breath indeed these hands have newly

stopped.

I know this act shows horrible and grim.

GRATIANO

Poor Desdemon, I am glad thy father's dead.

Thy match was mortal to him, and pure grief   245

Shore his old thread in twain. Did he live now,

This sight would make him do a desperate turn,

Yea, curse his better angel from his side,

NOTES

And fall to reprobance.

OTHELLO

'Tis pitiful. But yet Iago knows   250

That she with Cassio hath the act of shame

A thousand times committed. Cassio confessed it,

And she did gratify his amorous works

With that recognizance and pledge of love

Which I first gave her. I saw it in his hand.   255

It was a handkerchief, an antique token

My father gave my mother.

EMILIA O God! O heavenly God!

IAGO

Zounds, hold your peace!

EMILIA 'Twill out, 'twill out. I peace?   260

No, I will speak as liberal as the north.

Let heaven and men and devils, let them all,

All, all, cry shame against me, yet I'll speak.

IAGO Be wise, and get you home.

He draws his sword.

EMILIA

I will not.   265

GRATIANO Fie, your sword upon a woman!

NOTES

EMILIA

O thou dull Moor, that handkerchief thou speak'st

  of

I found by fortune, and did give my husband—

For often, with a solemn earnestness   270

(More than indeed belonged to such a trifle),

He begged of me to steal 't.

IAGO Villainous whore!

EMILIA

She give it Cassio? No, alas, I found it,

And I did give 't my husband.   275

IAGO Filth, thou liest!

EMILIA

By heaven, I do not, I do not, gentlemen!

To Othello. O murd'rous coxcomb, what should

  such a fool

Do with so good a wife?   280

OTHELLO Are there no stones in heaven

But what serves for the thunder?—Precious villain!

The Moor runs at Iago but is disarmed.

Iago kills his wife.

NOTES

GRATIANO

The woman falls! Sure he hath killed his wife.

EMILIA

Ay, ay! O, lay me by my mistress' side.   *Iago exits.*

GRATIANO He's gone, but his wife's killed.   285

MONTANO

'Tis a notorious villain. Take you this weapon

Which I have here recovered from the Moor.

Come, guard the door without. Let him not pass,

But kill him rather. I'll after that same villain,

For 'tis a damnèd slave.   290

Montano and Gratiano exit.

OTHELLO I am not valiant neither,

But every puny whipster gets my sword.

But why should honor outlive honesty?

Let it go all.

EMILIA What did thy song bode, lady?   295

Hark, canst thou hear me? I will play the swan

And die in music.

She sings.   *Willow, willow, willow.*

Moor, she was chaste. She loved thee, cruel Moor.

So come my soul to bliss, as I speak true.   300

NOTES

So speaking as I think, alas, I die.   *She dies.*

OTHELLO

I have another weapon in this chamber.

It is a sword of Spain, the ice brook's temper.

O, here it is.—Uncle, I must come forth.

GRATIANO, *within*

If thou attempt it, it will cost thee dear;   305

Thou hast no weapon and perforce must suffer.

OTHELLO

Look in upon me, then, and speak with me,

Or naked as I am I will assault thee.

Enter Gratiano.

GRATIANO

What is the matter?

OTHELLO Behold, I have a weapon.   310

A better never did itself sustain

Upon a soldier's thigh. I have seen the day

That with this little arm and this good sword

I have made my way through more impediments

Than twenty times your stop. But—O vain boast!—   315

NOTES

Who can control his fate? 'Tis not so now.

Be not afraid, though you do see me weaponed.

Here is my journey's end, here is my butt

And very sea-mark of my utmost sail.

Do you go back dismayed? 'Tis a lost fear.   320

Man but a rush against Othello's breast,

And he retires. Where should Othello go?

He looks toward the bed.

Now, how dost thou look now? O ill-starred wench,

Pale as thy smock, when we shall meet at compt,

This look of thine will hurl my soul from heaven,   325

And fiends will snatch at it. Cold, cold, my girl?

Even like thy chastity.—O cursèd, cursèd slave!—

Whip me, you devils,

From the possession of this heavenly sight!

Blow me about in winds, roast me in sulfur,   330

Wash me in steep-down gulfs of liquid fire!

O Desdemon! Dead, Desdemon! Dead! O, O!

Enter Lodovico, Cassio in a chair, Montano, and Iago,

with Officers.

NOTES

LODOVICO

Where is this rash and most unfortunate man?

OTHELLO

That's he that was Othello. Here I am.

LODOVICO

Where is that viper? Bring the villain forth.   335

Iago is brought forward.

OTHELLO

I look down towards his feet; but that's a fable.—

If that thou be'st a devil, I cannot kill thee.

He stabs Iago.

LODOVICO

Wrench his sword from him.

Othello is disarmed.

IAGO I bleed, sir, but not killed.

OTHELLO

I am not sorry neither. I'd have thee live,   340

For in my sense 'tis happiness to die.

LODOVICO

O thou Othello, that wert once so good,

Fall'n in the practice of a damnèd slave,

What shall be said to thee?

NOTES

OTHELLO Why, anything. 345

An honorable murderer, if you will,

For naught I did in hate, but all in honor.

LODOVICO

This wretch hath part confessed his villainy.

Did you and he consent in Cassio's death?

OTHELLO Ay. 350

CASSIO

Dear general, I never gave you cause.

OTHELLO

I do believe it, and I ask your pardon.

Will you, I pray, demand that demi-devil

Why he hath thus ensnared my soul and body?

IAGO

Demand me nothing. What you know, you know. 355

From this time forth I never will speak word.

LODOVICO What? Not to pray?

GRATIANO Torments will ope your lips.

OTHELLO Well, thou dost best.

LODOVICO Sir, 360

You shall understand what hath befall'n,

Which, as I think, you know not. Here is a letter

NOTES

Found in the pocket of the slain Roderigo,

And here another. *He shows papers.* The one of

  them imports   365

The death of Cassio, to be undertook

By Roderigo.

OTHELLO

O villain!

CASSIO Most heathenish and most gross.

LODOVICO

Now here's another discontented paper   370

Found in his pocket, too; and this it seems

Roderigo meant t' have sent this damnèd villain,

But that, belike, Iago in the interim

Came in and satisfied him.

OTHELLO O, thou pernicious caitiff!—   375

How came you, Cassio, by that handkerchief

That was my wife's?

CASSIO I found it in my chamber.

And he himself confessed it but even now,

That there he dropped it for a special purpose   380

Which wrought to his desire.

NOTES

OTHELLO O fool, fool, fool!

CASSIO

There is besides, in Roderigo's letter,

How he upbraids Iago, that he made him

Brave me upon the watch, whereon it came   385

That I was cast. And even but now he spake,

After long seeming dead: Iago hurt him,

Iago set him on.

LODOVICO, *to Othello*

You must forsake this room and go with us.

Your power and your command is taken off,   390

And Cassio rules in Cyprus. For this slave,

If there be any cunning cruelty

That can torment him much and hold him long,

It shall be his. You shall close prisoner rest,

Till that the nature of your fault be known   395

To the Venetian state.—Come, bring away.

OTHELLO

Soft you. A word or two before you go.

I have done the state some service, and they

know 't.

No more of that. I pray you in your letters,   400

NOTES

When you shall these unlucky deeds relate,

Speak of me as I am. Nothing extenuate,

Nor set down aught in malice. Then must you speak

Of one that loved not wisely, but too well;

Of one not easily jealous, but being wrought,   405

Perplexed in the extreme; of one whose hand,

Like the base Judean, threw a pearl away

Richer than all his tribe; of one whose subdued

   eyes,

Albeit unused to the melting mood,   410

Drops tears as fast as the Arabian trees

Their medicinable gum. Set you down this.

And say besides, that in Aleppo once,

Where a malignant and a turbanned Turk

Beat a Venetian and traduced the state,   415

I took by th' throat the circumcisèd dog,

And smote him, thus.   *He stabs himself.*

LODOVICO O bloody period!

GRATIANO All that is spoke is marred.

OTHELLO, *to Desdemona*

I kissed thee ere I killed thee. No way but this,   420

Killing myself, to die upon a kiss.   *He dies.*

NOTES

CASSIO

This did I fear, but thought he had no weapon,

For he was great of heart.

LODOVICO, *to Iago* O Spartan dog,

More fell than anguish, hunger, or the sea,   425

Look on the tragic loading of this bed.

This is thy work.—The object poisons sight.

Let it be hid.—Gratiano, keep the house,

And seize upon the fortunes of the Moor,

For they succeed on you. *To Cassio.* To you, lord   430

   governor,

Remains the censure of this hellish villain.

The time, the place, the torture, O, enforce it.

Myself will straight aboard, and to the state

This heavy act with heavy heart relate.   435

They exit.

NOTES

Printed in Great Britain
by Amazon

82474593R00125